A LONG ROAD TO FREEDOM

A LONG ROAD TO FREEDOM

The Life of Patrick Mc Crystal

Mary Mc Cartan

authorHOUSE®

AuthorHouse™
1663 Liberty Drive
Bloomington, IN 47403
www.authorhouse.com
Phone: 1-800-839-8640

This story is written from the thoughts and memories of a ninety-one year old veteran and although Patrick had a very acute memory, this book is not intended to be a historical document. It is simply the life story, of a man living during the events of history and his personal viewpoint of those experiences.

First published by AuthorHouse   06/13/2011

ISBN: 978-1-4567-8119-4 (sc)
ISBN: 978-1-4567-8120-0 (ebk)

Printed in the United States of America

Any people depicted in stock imagery provided by Thinkstock are models, and such images are being used for illustrative purposes only.

Certain stock imagery © Thinkstock.

This book is printed on acid-free paper.

Contents

This book is dedicated to the memory of:
My wonderful wife, Mary.

My beautiful daughter, Geraldine.

My comrades, lost in Malta, Leros, Palestine and Germany
during World War Two.

And to all innocent victims of war, all over the world, who paid
a price for someone else's idealism.

Acknowledgements

After years of silence, I thank my grandniece, Mary Mc Cartan, for recording my memories and deeply held emotional thoughts. She delved inside my head over the last few years to find my story, as well as painstakingly researching the facts. Thank you for believing in and respecting an old veteran. We have travelled on an emotional rollercoaster together, taking the risks and beat the odds. We are forever spiritually linked, regardless of the gaps of time, space or generation.

I want to thank my wonderful and precious daughters: Patricia, Kate and Rosemary. We have suffered so much together over the last few years, but we have always turned to the light of faith, to support us through the dark times. We will forever have laughter and the bright side of our memories to see us through adversity. I love you each dearly and thank you for your generous loving respect and care. I thank my precious grandchildren and great-grandchildren, you make my life worthwhile. When I look at our large family portrait I think that this family could not have exist, without my survival during the war. Many of my friends were denied the legacy of a family. I thank God for you and the babies still to come. I hope you understand and enjoy the freedom that so many of my generation suffered or died to secure for you. That freedom is my legacy to you all and I love each individual one of you. I especially wish to credit Rosemary and Peter with supporting and realising my dream of returning to Malta in 2010. It turned out to be a great worry and sacrifice for you both, but you made this man very happy. And to Kate and Patricia I say "Thank you" for your attentive nursing on my return home.

Thanks to my sons-in-law, Peter, Gerry, Mark and Paul. Thank you for your loving support and contribution to the McCrystal family over the years. To my sister, Mary Elizabeth Cheney, who has been my closest friend throughout my life and to our youngest brother, Gerry in London. Thanks also to my nephew, Owen, and grandnephew, Eugene McCrystal for documenting my story on film for future generations to see.

Thanks to Jonathan Maguire and the Royal Irish Fusiliers Museum in Armagh. I greatly appreciate your professionalism and research facilities. Thanks to Roger Castillo in Malta, Joe O'Loughlin in Belleek, Ruth Daly in Newtownbutler, AnnaB McCabe in Longford and Brendan Murray in Galway for proof reading the manuscript and offering your expert advice. Thanks to Valerie, Elaine, Pheme, Mary & Roslyn for your creative guidance.

Thanks to the exceptional staff at the Mater Dei Hospital, Malta for making the recovery from my critical illness so easy and comfortable. I believe I was in the right place at the right time and among the right people. And thanks also to my German Doctor Stefan Struebind, who accompanied me on the flight home from Malta in 2010.

I want to thank the little German family who took me into their home on the night of my escape in May 1945. I have no way of tracing you, as I am not even sure which village I was in, but you are always in my prayers.

Most importantly, I want to acknowledge and thank everyone who supported my family during the aftermath of the Omagh Bomb. Each individual prayer and deed sent to us either individually as a family, or to the collective community of Omagh, was recognised and appreciated. World leaders, pop-stars, actors and ordinary people from all over the world held us in their hearts and prayers, helping us to hold on and survive. You were the angels of hope shining a light for us to follow during the darkest of days. Thank you one and all.

Preface

The decision to write this book has come after 68 years of silence about many of the most traumatic events of Packie's life. He had decided to keep quiet in order to protect himself and his family from harm or narrow-minded bigotry in the highly emotive, divided community of Northern Ireland. Keeping his head down was the price he had to pay for daring to cross the line in his youth and he still feels anxious, even in 2010 about relating his past. In his early nineties his ambition to leave a legacy finally surpassed that fear. All his life he had been shy, avoiding attention and a little afraid of standing out in a crowd. Yet he was confident, full of fun and very self-assertive. Packie suddenly realised that his life was important and that his story needed to be heard. At last he realised that all he had experienced was for a purpose, so with the uniqueness of his maturity and a clear memory, his story of war comes pure, without the inflated bravado of youth. His story has not been tarnished by the years of embellished reciting of a hero's story to an appreciative audience. Packie's story has been protected in a safe cocoon of humility and silence, only nourished by a compassionate, intelligent and reflective heart and mind. He did not want to elaborate on gory details of battle or military logistics, as he simply wanted young people to hear the individual close-up account of the sufferings of war instead of always romancing in the satellite view of heroes and one-sided victory. He believed that it is important to understand that with every winner comes a defeated loser who is angry and eventually eager for revenge whether in their lifetime or by ensuring that the vendetta is past down to the next generations. Therefore if we use emotions instead of intelligence to correct the wrongs of the past we will never get off the roundabout of revenge, which ultimately sparks war. If we all understood our emotional inheritance we could control our common passion for justice in a more intelligent and constructive manner. We all have more in common than to we think and all sides suffer in the conflict of war.

The Author

I never considered myself a writer or imagined that I could some day write a book, but the inspiration for this first publication comes after the persistent request of a very special man. Patrick Mc Crystal came into my life only a few years ago, while I was on a search for a broken family link. My father had grown up as an orphan, left in a workhouse as a baby, until his mother found a good foster home for him before she married and moved away. He never saw his mother again and she died in 1989. Her name was Gertrude McCrystal, Patrick's stepsister. My father was born in late 1937, so Patrick did not know of his existence as he had already left home to join the army at that time, but he came looking for my father in 1995.

It was not until I became curious about my unknown, mysterious grandmother that I really became acquainted with Patrick. We instantly clicked with each other, as if we had always been connected. A forty-year old woman and an eighty-eight year old man found a healing link in the broken chain of our family. Not long after our meeting, Patrick asked me to write his story as he thought I understood him. When he revealed an army history I was intrigued, but I had no ambition or confidence for writing, never mind attempt a war novel. Instead I organised for a video interview with Packie to tell his own story and I moved on with my busy life as a businesswoman and mother. But he asked me in earnest, numerous times until I realised his urgency in May

2010 and I embarked on this amazing emotional journey with a man I have grown to love and admire. We became very close, as if we were the same spirit in a way. I knew the risk I was taking with my heart and that I would lose him all too soon, but I am so glad we travelled a little of our life path together and we are now eternally linked. He believed in truth and healing and our friendship epitomised that in a family that had borne so much pain and exclusion. During Patrick's last night on this earth, I sat with him all night long, holding his hand, alongside our cousin Noel Maguire. How strange that, after a whole lifetime of isolation, the separated McCrystal family would find each other! As the three of us held hands that night we knew our ancestors were satisfied and Packie's good work on this earth was complete. Families can be very cruel to each other, but they are the foundation to learning about acceptance, tolerance and forgiveness before we even attempt to heal the world. Patrick knew this and strived for peace within his family, community, nation and the world. He certainly has challenged my perceptions of this world by introducing me to the multi-faceted view of what being Irish and being free is about. In 2010, I attended my first Remembrance Day service in Malta. In my wildest imagination I could never have pictured myself standing in tears at a Remembrance Sunday event, praying for the heroes of a war that occurred long before I was born and until two years ago I had no emotional link with the suffering inflicted by that war. I have since learned that most families in Ireland have someone connected with the world wars. Growing up within a Nationalist tradition in Northern Ireland during the Troubles, it was incomprehensible to imagine that anyone I knew had served in the British Army and those Poppy Day events had nothing to do with me. But during the Catholic service in the magnificent cathedral in Valletta, surrounded by people from all over the world, I realised how passionately the rest of the world cherish the freedom they enjoy at the expense of the millions of lives sacrificed in war. Patrick McCrystal has taught me so much about acceptance and forgiveness within my own life. And I now believe that truth will always be revealed if we have the patience to wait.

Mary McCartan

Chapter One

A BURIED MEMORY

The old saying, "What doesn't kill you makes you stronger," is possibly very true and it certainly instills a great sense of bravery and endurance. But, regardless of the newfound strength that survival bestows, it also bequeaths a cautiousness that no doubt influences the survivor's future decisions. So in my case, it is understandable, that when a man has experienced many of the great traumas and horrors that this world can throw at him, he becomes very content to settle down to a quiet life and to try to forget the appalling destruction and deplorable evil, humankind can wreak upon each other.

My name is Patrick McCrystal. In 1998, I was a seventy-nine year old, retired engineer, still living my quiet life, in a modest home on the outskirts of a town called Omagh. It had seemed like a good decision to settle in my home county of Tyrone, to raise my family, within my Irish culture, with its rich traditions and strong sense of community. Omagh was by no means a cosmopolitan place, like the amazing cities I frequented as a young man on my travels, but it was a busy trading hub and a home to about eighteen thousand people. Most importantly, as far as I was concerned, this place was insignificant on the international radar of strategic war targets, located just within the rural western border of Northern Ireland and only a few miles from the most westerly shores of Europe. Omagh had remained a relatively peaceful place, even during the last thirty years of armed conflict in the north of Ireland. During those years, as many other towns had become economic and political black spots, Omagh had survived, as a thriving industrial town, with regional government employment opportunities and a healthy agricultural economy. Being situated seventy miles west of Belfast, the town lay along a busy national route, linking the rural northwest with Dublin, one hundred and ten miles to the south.

Omagh had developed over many centuries, as a natural meeting place for trade, at the point where the waters of the Drumragh and Camowen rivers merge, to form the River Strule. Nestling comfortably along the banks of the three meandering rivers, the town lay so low on the rich fertile river plain; it was almost hidden from the outside world, by the gently rising mounds of patchwork fields and random woodlands. The landscape of Tyrone reminded me of a quilt of many shades of green, draped over the valleys and rolling foothills, which gently rose up into the purple, yellow and brown shades of the peat and gorse clad hillsides, all bowing under the shadow of the breathtaking Sperrin mountains. Only the two French-gothic spires of the Catholic Sacred Heart Church, alongside the singular spire of St. Columba's Church of Ireland, betrayed the presence of a settlement among those enriched hills of gold and Neolithic treasures. Yes, there is gold in the Sperrin mountains and our ancestors had left numerous Megalith structures dotted around the Tyrone landscape. To add to this beautiful scene, the prevailing Atlantic rainclouds continuously traversed the sun, casting rainbows and waves of dancing shadows and beams of sunlight across the multi-coloured landscape. I had been exiled from this land during my youth, but my dreams had always carried me back to this familiar place and hopes of returning kept me from insanity during some of the darkest moments of my life. This beautiful landscape was deeply embedded in my mind's eye, as I imagined myself fishing in the river or walking through the fields of my childhood memories.

Despite the fact, that I have resided within the town limits of Omagh for almost fifty years now, I was a country boy at heart, with my family roots firmly fixed, some six miles upstream from Omagh, along the Camowen riverbank, near the village of Beragh. As an older man, I now had more time to reflect on the past and I realised that the river had always been a dominant feature in the McCrystal family, with their long history of milling corn and flax. My ancestors had survived on that landscape along the river for centuries, enduring the harshness of famine, war and oppression, until 1957, when my siblings and I buried my father in Beragh graveyard, next to my mother, and we all decided to move on from that tough, rural existence of our youth. My brothers went to England, my sister lived in Belfast and I returned to the easier life I had created in town. All the people who knew me from my childhood, in the countryside of Beragh, had called me Packie, but in my new life in town, I became known as Paddy. I shared that easy new life with my wonderful wife Mary until 1998, the year we celebrated fifty years of marriage. Our married life had been great and we fully appreciated the value of being healthy and happy, nourished by our four beautiful daughters and the sound of grandchildren running through our home.

When I first met Mary O' Donnell, more than fifty years before, she had instantly bestowed a feeling of calm security in my heart, just like a ship offered shelter in a harbour, after years adrift on the high seas. Her gentle presence reassured me, that I had finally found a safe haven, from a crazy world and her love distracted my mind from the nightmares of the past, a past that still dominated my dreams at the time. Ever since I had returned home from the war, I had tried to get over the brutality I had witnessed, by burying my emotions deep within and presenting a brave face to the outside world. With Mary I felt all was right with the world again and I could move on. Granted, my youth had been by-passed, but nothing could stop my determination to enjoy the future and I just knew the best was yet to come. So, having lived adrift until 1948, at twenty-eight years of age I asked Mary to marry me and I permitted my new life to commence. There was no necessity for a beautiful girl like Mary, to be exposed to the details of my past, so I talked very little about my youth. It was the future that interested me and I knew that, with her innocent strength by my side, I had the recipe and ingredients to create a protective family home and I spent the rest of my years striving for peace and harmony in our lives. Love and trust enfolded our home in contentment, while togetherness and fun filled our house with laughter.

Joining the workforce of the Post Office, as a telephone engineer, brought an additional stability to our home. As an engineer, I enjoyed my work during the post war technological era of the 1950's, a time when the telephone lines began to weave their way along the town streets and country roads, bringing the outside world closer. My career was particularly interesting, coinciding with the dawn of new telecommunication technology, such as fibre optic cables and electronic equipment and although I reached retirement age in 1984, I continued to take an interest in modern gadgets, an interest I hold until this very day. My time was completely occupied between work and home and so a lifetime passed by quickly, with me wrapped in Mary's loving devotion, and she in mine.

By 1998, I had a comfortable pension, a soft bed at night, my thriving vegetable garden and beautiful flowers surrounding my world. Possibly, the most important gift in my life was the fact that hunger never came to my door again, a fact, I never took for granted, but enjoyed, and thanked God for every bite I received every day of my life. Three of our daughters lived nearby and called on us almost daily, to share their stories and concerns. Kate had one daughter, Patricia had four, and Geraldine had one son. Our oldest girl, Rosemary was married and living in England, with her three boys, but with the telephone and air travel, they were never far away. So I only had one of my four grandsons living in Ireland and we needed each other for moral support. I was glad to have another male battling for mercy with me, against the might of my wife, my daughters and five granddaughters. The females were all wonderfully gentle individuals, but together they were quite a force. Secretly I enjoyed their attention, but I must say, the addition of a busy social life with my mates, revolving around the local parish community centre with competitive games of darts or bowls and great sporting debates, complemented my female-dominated home life.

It was a fairly normal existence for a retired man and I'm sure any of my neighbours of the time would have said: "What does Paddy know about life or the worries of the world? Sure hadn't he it easy, with a good job and a wife and daughters dancing attention on him all his life. "Well, that may have been the story people assumed about my life and I was extremely happy to portray that image of a lighthearted soul. In fact it was almost the truth, as wee Paddy really did enjoy every moment of the good times and had no difficulty facing each new morning with enthusiasm. Life was great.

I had lived most of the years of my life in this relatively peaceful, normal community. I went to Mass, completed an honest day's work for an honest day's pay, I helped my neighbours any way I could and I was a well-loved father and grandfather. What more can a man want? Is there really any other measure of true success? Our grandchildren gave us so much enjoyment and Mary and I loved them all so much. My eyes danced with pride as I, more than most people, knew the value of the love and safety that surrounded my life.

Yet, I was still always a little on guard, always on the look out for what was going on behind me. I knew there was a price to be paid, a price for inattentiveness, but I told no one of the horrors my boyhood eyes had seen. In the years of my youth I had watched so many other young men pay the price for dropping their guard, but those pictures remained confined, safe in my head, carefully managed and with the distance of time, I had almost convinced myself that it was not me at all who had lived in those horrific scenes more than fifty years before. I had decided a long time ago that I had a choice, a choice to either manage those thoughts, or surrender to insanity along with many of my wartime comrades. My decision to remain sane, with the assistance of a strong faith, had paid off thus far as I had survived when many men had not. I had played my part in the world of war, protecting my homeland from ever having to experience the brutality, suffering and extermination policies of the Nazi regime. Most of the civilian populations of Europe had been forced to experience these policies first hand, causing extreme desolation and forever altering the culture of each affected nation.

The memory of living in that wasteland of rubble and human massacre still turns the blood in my veins to ice and the acid in my stomach into a burning, gnawing pain deep within me. Witnessing war, up close and personal, had taught me never to underestimate the power of hatred on all sides of a conflict. The crimes of the Nazis against the innocent millions of Europeans has been well documented and I experienced that brutality first hand, but I had also witnessed the destruction of the ordinary German people as they suffered at the hands of, not only their own countrymen, but also our own Allied armies. In war there maybe two sides, but everyone suffers, especially the people in the middle ground with no side to protect them. No matter how neutral or passive your resolve may be, when war pushes its ugly face up against yours, it will do everything it can to force your hand and pick a side; otherwise, it simply crushes you in between.

But, during the Second World War, the Nazis did not even give many ordinary people the choice of joining a side. In their own country they systematically eradicated the Jews, the handicapped children, the mentally ill or physically infirm, the Gypsies, the Slovaks; the list just kept extending. The criteria of sub-human status widened to include more people as Hitler's forces invaded Austria, Poland, France, Holland, Italy, the Balkans, Greece and Norway and started pushing into Africa, Russia and almost breached the shores of Britain. Nazi records revealed a detailed invasion plan for Ireland called "Operation Green", which contained information about our towns and villages throughout the whole island with no regard to the border, and I often wondered how the Irish nation would have fared under their regime. Would any of us have been considered pure enough for their master race? History saved us that discovery and left us here to fight that question out among ourselves. No-one knows what might have been, since either right or wrong, I alongside many thousands of Irishmen, in the British Army, helped prevent that mayhem from reaching the shores of Ireland, but paid a huge personal price in the process. I immediately realised on returning home, that no one here wanted to see the receipt or hear my story. In the context of the politics of this small island, I may have joined the wrong army, but in a worldwide context the view was very different.

Back in 1945, no one in my Irish Nationalist community had any interest in a returning British Army solider. In fact, as the years rolled on towards "The Troubles" in Northern Ireland, it might have been downright suicidal for me to reveal my army history. Instead, I quietly melted back into the culture I was born and raised in. I knew very well the strategy of survival; I needed to be home among the people I loved and understood, having been in exile among strangers and terror for most of my youth, but in order to create a safe haven for my family, the past had to be denied. And, as the years rolled by, I never found an opportunity, nor any reason, to describe those terrible years to the innocent, trusting people about me.

I wisely hid away my precious medals of honour and I hid the painful memories of that episode of my life behind my playful, devilish eyes, and lived my life.

A good long contented life.

Chapter Two

AN AUGUST DAY

During the early months of 1998, the people of Northern Ireland had much to look forward to as, that year, a ceasefire was established after thirty years of bloody conflict. The history of Ireland is a tragic and complicated story, but in brief, Northern Ireland in 1998 was made up of "The Six Counties" that had remained under British rule when the Republic of Ireland gained independence in 1921. The communities in the North were divided into two main groups with extreme views held by some within both factions, but with many people quietly occupying the moderate middle ground. The Irish Nationalists, who were generally Roman Catholics, wished to be reunited with the rest of Ireland. The British Unionists, predominantly Protestants, wanted Northern Ireland to remain within the United Kingdom and, as the majority; they had the power and government support to maintain the Union. The opposition to the union and the resolute defense of it, created "The Troubles" as each side fueled the hatred with appalling words and horrifying deeds for decades.

In early 1998, after all that hurt and misery, the sides were finally willing to sit down together and the "Good Friday Agreement" between all the opposing political parties was signed. There was the hope of establishing a devolved power-sharing government, following years of direct rule from London and for the first time in many years, a foundation for lasting stability and equality was in sight.

But as summer approached sporadic attacks and tit-for-tat incidents were reported and a car bomb had exploded in the town of Banbridge with thirty-five people injured. Extreme dissident groups on both sides remained unhappy as some viewed the agreement as a blockage to an all-Ireland reunification and the other side felt it loosened the bond with the United Kingdom. July was always a hot spot month in the North anyway because of the parades to commemorate protestant William of Orange's victory over the catholic King James in 1690. This year was particularly difficult, as an ongoing issue about a contentious Parade at Drumcree, on the Gravaghey Road in Portadown, had flared into a horrific situation in July culminating in the death of three very young children of a mixed religious family. The three innocent brothers were killed, when a firebomb was thrown at their house, in revenge over a banned parade. I wondered how the human right, to march down a road, was worth the precious lives of a young family? But all this was to be expected in Northern Ireland, as our past history had always been the weapon used against our future. As August rolled in, people hoped things would settle down again.

Our community in Omagh was complacent in the August summer sun of 1998. The barricades and army checkpoints were disappearing and the town was busy these days with tourists and teenagers out and about on their holidays. From mid-August, families started preparing for the return to school with the search for uniforms, shoes and schoolbags and on Saturday the 15th August, the weather was lovely after a fairly wet summer, so it was a great day for a trip to town in the sunshine. My teenage granddaughters had gone to look around the shops together and my daughter, Geraldine worked in a town centre drapery shop so I could be assured she was at work during this busy retail season. My wife Mary and I had spent that morning about the house. August is a wonderful month for the garden, as the potatoes can be dug for the dinner, the cabbage, peas, beans, tomatoes and such are ready for harvesting and then can be stored or frozen. I make my own jams with the fruit, so I was always pushed to get enough hours in the day to complete all the tasks. As usual, Mary made bread and went about her normal chores around the house. On a Saturday evening we could expect some of the girls and the grandchildren to call in, before or after Mass, so Mary liked to have something nice ready for their tea. She was a great baker and we all loved her cakes and fresh bread.

I had always enjoyed Saturdays, but that day I felt different. In fact I had been unsettled all week, with a feeling of doom in the pit of my stomach. A feeling I hadn't felt for many years. Hadn't I said to Geraldine the night before on the phone, "I don't like to see this August weekend" and when she asked, "Why?" I answered, "Well you know that all our people died in August, well the most of them anyway and I don't like it at all." What had possessed me to say such a thing to our Geraldine? I had never said anything like that before, but I knew something was wrong. Geraldine had rang us every night since she got married and that night she was late because she had visitors in. I had been waiting for her call to voice my uneasiness, but her light-hearted soul hardly heard me. She knew my father, brothers, uncle and stepsister had all died in August, but she could see no relevance in that and convinced me to relax. It was still on my mind to call over to Geraldine in the morning to tell her to be careful but I never did, because, as I was walking out of the driveway to go, a neighbour stopped and offered me a lift to 11am Mass, so I went there instead. The 15th of August is the feast day of the Assumption of Our Lady into Heaven, so Catholics usually celebrate by going to Mass. By lunchtime, I still had it on my mind, but for some reason I just hadn't the power to go into town. I didn't understand what I was feeling myself, so how could I explain it to someone else. Maybe I thought my fear might have sounded crazy. Anyway, Geraldine would have stayed on at her work despite anything I said. She just loved her work.

The girls often laughed at me for being too cautious or worrisome. I liked to sit with my back to the wall, so as not to leave myself in a vulnerable position where people could approach me from behind. I ensured we always had a good supply of food in the larder and the oil, gas and batteries did not run low. Don't get me wrong; otherwise I am a lighthearted relaxed guy who loves socializing, but I just need to know the lay of the land, so to speak. I was protective of my girls growing up, yet let them run on and enjoy life. I can only remember one other occasion that I felt that same sense of doom as I was feeling that Saturday. One day, in the late seventies our youngest daughter Patricia, then just a teenager, was going to a dance in Bundoran, a seaside town about 45 miles away on the other side of the border. There was a military checkpoint at the border, but the young ones were well accustomed to negotiating their way through those. The band playing that night were the very popular Celtic rock heartthrobs, Horslips and Patricia was so excited about the opportunity to see them in a live concert. As she and her friend stood on the doorstep that evening talking to me, a strange effect appeared around their heads and I was so overwhelmed that I immediately told them I had a bad feeling and asked them not to go. Of course they all laughed at me and ran on, but that night Patricia's friend was killed off the back of a motorbike. Thank God I did not feel like that very often, but that August weekend, it was the same feeling in my stomach for sure.

On returning from the Church, Mary and I had lunch and we tidied up together. Even though I had retired as a telephone engineer fifteen years earlier, I still kept myself busy every day. Without fail, I woke at seven in the morning and I never experienced one boring moment until retiring to bed at midnight. But, the sports channel on a Saturday afternoon was my special time and I could get engrossed in all the sporting action, and so at 2pm I sat down as usual to watch the horse racing on the television. In my younger days, I placed the odd bet on a big race or two with my workmates, but now I just enjoyed predicting winners and listening to the analysis by the commentators. I suppose I had inherited a love of horses from my father and also his keen eye for quality. He had worked with farm horses all his life and somehow instinctively I could eye up the horses and pick the winners. That afternoon I was confident about my favorites, so I settled in to be proven an expert yet again, if only in my own head. This hour proved to be a time of calm and contentment just before the storm, as somewhere in the distance, the clouds of doom were rolling into Omagh within the hearts of evil men.

It happened suddenly, yet quietly, at about ten minutes past three in the afternoon as I sat in my comfortable armchair in front of the television. Firstly, the back door of the house blew open into the kitchen and then I heard the distant boom of a bomb blast, an old familiar sound, a little like thunder yet different. I froze. The noise was barely audible over the television, but I did not have to ask, "What was that?" I knew very well what it was; as my stomach told me, every muscle in my body told me, it was a bomb.

How can I explain the sensation of terror to someone who has never experienced it? Maybe the feeling is different for each person, but mine felt like every nerve ending in my body was suddenly put on high alert and the moment of time just slowed down. The reality of the moment became like a slow motion movie that faded to the background, while the thoughts in my head started running at high speed as the main picture show. In that one short moment, so much can flash through your mind, so many memories, so many possible scenarios and in just a flash of a moment, I was displaced in time and space to somewhere else, somewhere long ago.

My immediate reaction was to duck before the next wave of bombers planes reached the shore. I could see the planes flying low over the blue Mediterranean Sea, hundreds of German Stuka 87's approaching the Maltese shoreline, glistening in the sunlight, like stars winking at me. I could feel the gun in my hand and the hot sun at my back, but I was powerless. Every cell in my body tingled, waiting for hell to rain down yet again. As the first bombs hit the ground, I felt the tremor and the screech of the planes startle me back to the reality of the present, just as quickly as I had left. My body trembled and as my horse crossed the finish line on the television I asked myself, "What on earth is wrong with you today Packie?"

I don't know why I reacted with such vivid memories this time, as Omagh had experienced bombs many times before. Maybe I was just getting too old to try and understand why people preferred to destroy the pathway to their freedom instead of building bridges to a solution. Anyway, the town would be cleared, tidied up in a few months and on we'd go. I was sure the Police were ready for this as there had been a car bomb in another town earlier that summer and there had been rumours that Omagh was on the list. Of course, it was distressing after so much political progress and hopes for lasting peace, but after thirty years of mayhem, you learn to get on with things. Disappointment, carnage and death were normal here so you think, "Ah well," I suppose things are back to normal again.

I got the strength to get up from my chair and go to the kitchen to check on Mary. She had been ironing while watching a black and white, John Wayne movie—she had no interest in the horses. We discussed the door that had blown open beside her as it had always been stiff to open and it was strange that it opened so easily with this blast nearly a mile away. Of course, we automatically knew the blast came from the town.

Maybe I should explain that bombs, shootings, riots and such were everyday news for most people in Northern Ireland during the Troubles. After thirty years we were experts. Everybody had great stories of near misses and our family was no exception. "Sure, do you remember the time our Geraldine got blown into the hedge by a bomb," was one of those stories, and we would all laugh. Even though this was a serious event, we knew how to shake it off, make a joke of it and move on. The point I am trying to make is that a person's perception of normal life is what a person is accustomed to everyday. But that incident really did happen sometime in the 1970's when Geraldine was about eighteen. We lived on the Derry Road, just half a mile from the town centre, so we all walked to work or school every day. One day Geraldine headed off walking to work with her usual enthusiasm. As she passed by our local corner shop, a bomb went off not far from the army camp entrance and she was blown off her feet and into the hedge. A local woman took her into her house and gave her a cup of tea and Geraldine went on to her work as normal.

Geraldine had always worked in town. Some years later she was employed in Mc Millan's Clothes shop and one Wednesday evening in May 1972, as the boss was leaving, she asked our Geraldine to wash all the glass top counters. Geraldine had set a boiling hot basin of water on the counter and the glass shattered. She was distraught when she came home, because she didn't know how she could face the boss the next morning. Anyway she need not have worried, as that night the IRA blew up a side street in Omagh called Scarffe's Entry and the blast sorted out all Mc Millan's glass counters. We all heard the explosion at about a quarter past mid-night, but we did not realise the damage caused by the car bomb until the next morning when we arrived in town for work. Geraldine was so relieved when she gazed at the shop counters and she said, "Well this is one thing I can thank the IRA for!" and she happily spent that day clearing up glass. She had a great spirit and made the best of every situation. That's the way we dealt with things generally in the North; no matter how bad things were, we'd try and see the bright side of it and there was always the opportunity for a joke about it.

As Mary and I were still debating about the back door, our youngest daughter, Patricia arrived. Her daughter Nicola and Kate's daughter, Joni, were in the town and they had just rung to say, they had been standing around the corner from the bombsite, but they were not hurt. The two girls had immediately run to the bus station to use the public telephone to ring home. A few minutes later, all the phone lines in the Omagh area shut down. I knew all the telephone cable pathways under and over the town and understood how a bomb could damage the network as I had laid many of those cables over the years. As everyone turned to their mobile phones, those networks became overloaded and within minutes all communication shut down. The phone networks remained unavailable that evening and there was complete chaos as no one could get information. Patricia was very upset as she came into our house to tell about the explosion. The girls were only fifteen years old and sounded very distraught on the phone, asking what they should do. Patricia had told them to come home immediately, so I was out on the street walking up and down waiting for them, along with all the neighbours, as more and more people came in from the town with reports of the devastation. Omagh has a long straight street, widening in a V-shape, as it rises up towards the dominating Courthouse at the top of the hill. The bomb had been placed at the lower end of the town, at the narrowest point between the buildings, for maximum effect.

All sorts of reports came from town, about people dead on the street and the buildings collapsing about them. We put on the radio for news, but the story was not good and all my senses could imagine the scene. I might as well have been there; I could see, feel, hear and smell it all. I think smell has the most lasting memory. I knew exactly what the reality was. How many of those scenes had I cleared in Malta? How many mates and innocent civilians had I found in that rubble? I knew the random choice of life an explosion makes. You die, you live, you lose a leg and you lose your sanity. I had dodged the lot time after time, blast after blast. I survived every time to look around through the smoke and dust, realizing I still existed with the chance to keep on breathing. I survived air raids, night and day, with thousands of bombs dropping around me for four solid years. The memory of this must have been the doom I was feeling all week, or maybe I had enough experience to practically smell that bomb making its journey towards Omagh.

I flashed back to reality. I had to pull myself together as my family knew little or nothing about my military experiences. I don't think the girls even knew I was in the army, never mind the war, so this was not a good time for me to breakdown or open that can of emotional worms. I recovered from this lapse of concentration and focused on the feeling of relief as my granddaughter Nicola finally came walking down the road, covered in dust, but intact. She told us Joni had also gone home to her parents, at the other side of town. They had helped injured people onto buses before making their way home. Why would my little girls have to see such a sight? I simply closed my eyes and shook my head as I realised that battle had found me again, only this time my loved ones were in the nightmare with me. I gave Nicola a tight hug and heaved a deep sigh of relief, then disgust as I caught the smell of her clothes, a smell that confirmed to me what sights her beautiful eyes must have absorbed. I knew my little girls were forever altered from the two innocent teenagers, who went laughing to town in the morning.

That afternoon, I was thinking that some families were going to have a hard time ahead of them, but Geraldine did not cross my mind at that time. She worked in Watterson's Drapery, situated at the top end of the town, closer to the Courthouse. She had no reason to be down the lower end of the street as her shop could be evacuated out the back towards the car parks. Watterson's was no stranger to bomb evacuations over the years, but actually only sustained a few direct hits. In 1978, on November 14th, a car-bomb exploded outside a butcher shop on Bridge Street. The exterior of Watterson's was badly damaged in that attack and five days later, an incendiary device was left in the ladies fashion department upstairs were Geraldine worked. Fire destroyed the first floor and water caused damage to the ground floor. In April, 1979, a car-bomb planted outside the nearby Allied Irish Bank in High Street, went off, causing yet more exterior damage. Yet again, at the heart of the Christmas rush, in 1983, the shop was devastated by a third car bomb placed outside the Royal Arms Hotel and the roof and windows were wrecked again. Thankfully, with all the attacks on Omagh town centre, no one had ever been killed.

Someone arrived from town and told me they had seen Geraldine and she was fine, so we concerned ourselves with the neighbours, waiting with them until their loved ones appeared or made contact. There was high tension, but I knew it was pointless trying to get into town, so we waited. What assistance could I, a seventy-nine year-old man offer in that mayhem, even though I probably had more experience of this kind of operation than most people, well most people still alive. Geraldine's husband, Mark, rang to ask if Geraldine had been in touch with us and, hearing that she hadn't, he said he would go looking for her at the shop. Next we heard that Geraldine had a leg wound and they had taken her to hospital to get stitches and that Mark was going to her. I suppose I should have realised then that all was not well, but I let myself believe what we had heard. I don't know whether I was in shock or just couldn't face it, but I didn't panic. The arrival of Kate, her husband, Gerry, and Joni brought some comfort and someone suggested recording Geraldine's favourite TV show as she might miss it in hospital. I suppose everyone was in shock and when people are in shock, they just want to do normal, familiar things.

Well, eventually I must have pulled my act together. The question, "How did Geraldine get a leg wound?" started to niggle in my head. Was she somewhere near the bomb? There was the realisation that all was not well and the thought sunk in slowly. No-one wanted to alarm the other, but gradually a dread seeped into the house. Our granddaughters had just started to calm down so we had to be careful not to make a fuss, but eventually Gerry ordered a taxi to take us to the hospital in Omagh. He said a taxi could bring us to the door without any parking problems. It must have been after six o' clock by this time, almost three hours after the bomb, three hours during which our brains had remained suspended in time. When the taxi arrived, it was decided that Mary, Kate and myself should go to see Geraldine. The local taxi men took everyone wherever they needed to go that day, free of charge, and the whole town was in confusion, with people running from place to place looking for family and friends. The local leisure centre had been converted into an information centre for relatives to come to check the lists of names received from the police and the hospitals.

The injured had been transferred to hospitals all over the north and relatives didn't know where to look or if they needed to be looking at all. Hundreds of people had been injured and the list was constantly up-dated from the busloads of injured arriving at different hospitals. With no telephone contact, uninjured people had returned home, while their relatives frantically searched the town, the hospitals or the lists. The army barracks became a makeshift mortuary, with a bus ferrying relatives back and forth from the leisure centre for identification of bodies, but we knew our girl was alive, so we went towards the Tyrone County Hospital.

The roads were busy with people driving around in a daze, as fire engines, ambulances, electricity and water service vehicles with flashing lights zoomed past, all alerting us to the fact that we existed in a state of intense anxiety. It was as if the atmosphere was electrified, as the hairs on my arms stood on end and a shiver ran through my whole being. Police had blocked off all the streets near the town centre, so we skirted around to avoid the roadblocks. The police were also stopping traffic up to the hospital, but they let our taxi through and all I can remember is the chaos that met us at the hospital door. Injured people sat or lay along the corridor floors, as every corner of each ward was crammed with patients. There was blood everywhere; so much blood that it was like entering an army field hospital, except for the presence of frantic relatives adding to the mayhem as they searched for loved ones. Mary and I wandered through the injured bodies asking blood-stained staff about Geraldine and we were eventually told she was in theatre getting stitches, so we couldn't see her. As we stood there paralyzed and helpless, I could have sworn I saw her on a trolley passing down the corridor, but I did not run after her, as I think I was afraid of what I might see. Most of the people were not identifiable, so maybe I was wrong. The white dust covering the face and hair of the victims gave them a ghostly appearance and, added to the injuries, familiar faces were rendered unrecognisable.

Then we heard talk that Geraldine was to be airlifted to Belfast at nine o' clock that night. We were desperate to see her, but with the staff so busy, we did not want to interfere. We are not pushy folk normally and the staff had enough problems that night without us shouting. I wish now I had demanded to see her before that airlift. We eventually found Geraldine's husband, Mark, and he said he would get her some pyjamas and things and go on to Belfast. We were going to wait at home. Well, that was the plan until a nurse asked my other daughter Kate about Geraldine's condition and Kate explained that she was fine but going to Belfast to get her leg sorted. The nurse seemed confused and asked if we had seen Geraldine. She then explained that Geraldine had been very ill when she attended her on the journey from the town and that maybe we should go to Belfast immediately.

We returned home for the car and I went to get Geraldine's son, Gareth, who was out kicking football with friends. Kate and I prepared to go to Belfast, leaving Patricia at home with her children and Mary with Gareth. Just as we were leaving the house we heard on the radio that another victim of the Omagh Bomb had just died in the Royal Victoria Hospital and Patricia calmly said, "You're too late, as our Geraldine is already dead." Sure enough, one hour and twenty minutes later when we arrived at the hospital in Belfast, some seventy miles away, we were met by the staff, given a cup of tea and told that our beautiful precious daughter was gone and our grandson left motherless.

It may sound a little stark, but it was as simple as that—no goodbyes. We would never see her smiling face again. The hospital staff treated us so kindly, even though their unit was filling up with major trauma victims as helicopter after helicopter arrived in from Omagh, but they gave us time and understanding. They listened as we questioned, "Why was Geraldine down that end of town?" "How could this be happening?" "Why had we not been allowed to see our own daughter in Omagh?" Nothing made sense at that time. We met those same nurses some months later at a remembrance event at Stormont Castle and they reassured us that they had held hands around Geraldine and prayed with the hospital chaplain as she died. It was a comfort to know she was not alone when we were unable to be there. The chaplain told me he had never witnessed such a beautiful event as Geraldine's passing, as hospital staff of all faiths gathered together, hand and hand, to pray for her on her final journey from this earth. We were never to see our daughter again as her body was already away to the morgue that night and the coffin was never opened.

In a way we were lucky, for we knew were we stood before the sun set on that feast day of the Assumption of Our Lady in 1998. Other families had to wait for confirmation of death for a few days, reliant on DNA for identification in some cases. We did not have the anguish of waiting. The final toll was thirty-one dead including unborn, eight-month term twins, young children, teenagers, tourists and locals, along with at least two hundred and forty injured. Many others were traumatized by the experience of the blast or the aftermath. Others who had treated or assisted the wounded suffered badly too and the situation in our community seemed like a black hole. That day had sucked every ounce of comprehension, resilience and hope from us. Our old tried and tested survival techniques failed us all at this final hurdle of the war. We believed there could never be a recovery, yet we did continue to survive. We planned our funerals, we visited each other's wake houses and shared condolences, we cleared up the mess and with the help of numbness, we continued breathing.

OUR GERALDINE

Chapter Three

A SECRET REVEALED

After a few days, Geraldine's coffin returned to Omagh to be waked in the new home she shared with her husband and son. She had lived with us until she was forty years old, and only two years previously, Geraldine had married Mark Breslin and set up a lovely home of their own. They were only starting out and I am sure they had so many dreams and plans. In Ireland, we still bring our dead home to the house for two days, before burial on the third day. Neighbours and friends come to visit and have tea with the family throughout the days and nights of the wake. This intensely busy time is very supportive for the family and enables everyone to tell their stories about the deceased and gently let the reality sink in. Thousands of people came to shake our hands and try to comfort us. A continuous queue of people filed through the house and extended down the street, just waiting to pay their respects during those two days and nights. Even the Bishop of Derry, came to the house to sympathise with us and we went to see other bereaved families to do the same. No matter what religion, we all shared the same pain, and those were dark days as the grim stories slowly revealed the facts.

There had been a warning received about a bomb near the courthouse, so the people in the shops and on the street had been sent down the town, away from the courthouse to wait for the all-clear. Little did they know that they had gathered around the bomb instead as the warning had been incorrect. We heard that Geraldine's workmates had been with her on the street and that her close friend, Ann McCombe was also dead, along with her colleague, Veda Short. Another colleague was seriously ill in hospital. We were told that Geraldine had been helping two children, who had become separated from their Mammy, so she walked them down the street and sent them to safety, along Scarffe's Entry, to the car parks away from the town. But somehow she herself ended up with the crowd at the bottom of the street, gathered around a car with a bomb in the boot. She had been dancing around in the crowd, lighted-hearted as ever, just waiting for the alert to be called off so that she could get back to work. Everybody knew Geraldine from the shop and as people filed through the house, we heard so many wonderful stories about her kindness. We had a few laughs also as we wondered if our style queen Geraldine would approve of the flowers or the clothes we were wearing. She had always been our family organizer and ensured everything and everybody looked good. We were lost without the boss to organise us all in this bizarre and chaotic family situation. We heard from emergency staff, that she had been very ill on the way to hospital and that there had been a young teenage fella with her, holding her hand on the street, but nobody knew who he was. Nobody knew who went in the helicopter with her or if she had spoken. I wanted to know if she had spoken. Had she been afraid? Why did she go down the town? I guess I will never know the answers.

One of the callers to the house was an old army colleague of mine, Walter Pancott. We were two of the few lads who returned home to Omagh after the war in 1945. Of the hundreds who left Omagh, I think less than fifteen lads returned. In the subsequent years, Walter and I had met up from time to time in the town, yet we never mentioned the war. I did not frequent the pubs often, but I did socialise an odd night with the boys from work, so occasionally Walter and I stood at the bar counter in the crowd waiting to be served and Walter would say something like, "Looks like you and me are back on the frontline again

McCrystal", but that was it, nothing else would be said. The war topic was taboo. Anyway, both Walter and I knew our service history was better off concealed, especially in the public houses in our neck of the woods, as neither of us wanted a black eye or worse. Despite our unique understanding of each other's history, Walter and I had not remained close friends so when he arrived at the wake house my family did not know him. I was at another victim's wake elsewhere when he walked in through the door, so my daughters spoke to him first and in the process of introducing himself, he blurted out something along the lines of, "Isn't it cruel your father has to lose a daughter like this, after all the bombing he has lived through himself." The girls didn't know what he was talking about and were shocked by Walter's revelations about my Second World War history.

It is a lesson about secrets. They always bide their time, but in the end, they come seeping out when you least expect it. And so, on top of our grief and shock about Geraldine, I found myself revealing my deeply held secret. It must have been a great shock to my darling girls, but it was a distraction I suppose, as over the next few years I unfolded the story I had tried to keep from them all my life. It was an ugly story of human destruction, a story I intended never to tell. My girls should've remained naïve about such evil, for hadn't I fought a war, over fifty years ago, giving up my own innocent youth, in the hope of a more peaceful future? I had persevered in rearing my family through a further thirty years of conflict in my own country and I had protected them by keeping my head down and my nose clean. In teaching them the same strategy, I had always preached tolerance and peace. So what had I done to deserve this? I had asked for nothing more than a quiet, safe life and I thought the conflict here was over and my countrymen had finally realised the futility of war. But here it was, right on my doorstep. War had found me again, knocking hard on the door of my family home. I was defeated and numb, never had I felt such a strong need to lay down and die.

But my family needed me, so despite the hopelessness and pain, I felt an old familiar soldier rise up from deep within me, determined to lighten the tension with a witty remark or two. It was my natural role within our platoon, to lift morale with a smart remark at the darkest moments of battle. A few of my commanding officers had warned me to keep a check on my tongue, but my mates always appreciated the jokes that possibly saved us from insanity in the most dire of situations.

Although so very much older now, I still had my razor sharp wit and despite the fact, that I was frozen with grief as a father, the old soldier in me knew how to take command of the situation and rally the troops. The destruction of that bomb in Omagh may have knocked us down, but I quickly asserted my determination that the evil malice it carried with it would not enter our souls. I knew the consequences of letting that happen, I had seen it before, when people let hurt turn to anger and thoughts of revenge go on to consume the mind. Of course, I realised that no matter how hard we try to eradicate that one dreadful attack from our mind, we will never undo the damage it caused, but I knew we needed to repel the evil intention carried with that bomb. The real intention is by far more powerful than the bomb itself. The intention is to incite hatred and revenge, enabling the evil to infiltrate the kindest of hearts, knowing that evil thrives on anger. Not only will it consume life at the time of the attack, anger will go on to eat up a whole lifetime if we let it. Yes, anger will slowly erase all the good memories of our lives until it finally leaves nothing but the misery, hopelessness and pain of that one destructive moment.

That can only happen if we give up on hope and faith. When standing at the abyss of despair, we humans have a choice; to turn to the light and grasp at the hand of hope, or to simply let our mind tip on over the edge into the darkness. Even then, angels will continue to reach for us if we choose to open our hearts, but anger and hurt likes to shut us off from others, in the fear of getting hurt again. My family needed to hear that it is possible to survive this kind of evil attack and I could show them how. Hadn't I successfully kept anger and hurt at bay in my head all my life? I have Walter to thank for reminding me that I had survived before. I suppose I could march us through this nightmare and, by whistling an old familiar marching tune, my natural survival instinct should kick in. "So pack up your troubles in your old kit bag and smile." I knew the path to guide my family along, one step at a time, that would lead them out of this devastation. It would be a long road, but it was better than lying down in the rumble and surrendering to evil's wishes. I had endured persecution against my soul too many times in the past to simply give up at this late stage and let anger destroy us.

Chapter Four

MY EARLY LIFE

I was born on April 16th 1919 in Brackey, a small townland in the Parish of Beragh. Our house was situated about six miles from Omagh, the county town of Tyrone, in Ireland. But I knew little about such a far away place as Omagh, because my world revolved around the little village of Beragh, only 2 miles away from our humble abode. With the school, the church and the shop all located there, Beragh was the centre of the universe while I was growing up. The island of Ireland was one unified country of thirty-two counties at the time I was born, though still under British rule. A raging war for Independence was fought during the first few years of my life, until a deal was negotiated with the British, in the form of a Treaty, for the establishment of a Free State. As part of the deal, the six most northeasterly counties of Ulster were to be enclosed by a border, to remain part of the United Kingdom of Great Britain, while the rest became the newly formed Free State of Ireland, established on December 6th 1922.

A bloody civil war ensued immediately after gaining independence, fought between Irish people who accepted the Treaty for independence of just twenty-six counties and those who wanted to fight on for total freedom of the whole island. It was a bitter war, pitting friend against friend, neighbour against neighbour and even brother against brother, leaving deep divisions within communities all over Ireland as each individual decided, what price they were willing to pay for freedom. I suppose it was a decision between accepting the deal on the table for peace's sake or risking the loss of more and more lives. Well, eventually the majority decided that they had suffered enough and the Treaty was generally accepted for the sake of peace, with only a few continuing to fight against it. The citizens of the new Free State or Eire as we called it, devoted their energy to building an independent infrastructure and government under a new flag, the tri-colour, with green for Nationalists, orange for Orangemen and white for peace between them. Meanwhile the north was reinforced within Britain under the Union Jack flag.

The people were war-weary on both sides of the border, which diminished the support for armed struggle. The IRA did continue that struggle for Irish unity, with varying intensity, over the next ninety years of my life, but generally, when the line was drawn on the Irish landscape in 1922 by the powers that be, most ordinary people had to adapt to finding a way to survive. Wherever they found themselves, taxes still had to be paid and families still needed food. I was only three years old when this all happened, so it made absolutely no difference to my life as a child. Times were hard no matter which side of the border you ended up on.

MAP OF IRELAND

Anyway, County Tyrone and therefore my family, remained part of the United Kingdom in the newly named "Northern Ireland," or "The Six Counties." Looking back now, it is clear to see how that imaginary geographical line, drawn in my childhood, did go on to significantly influence and affect my later life. That border, drawn at the time of my birth as a compromise to bring peace, incited so much anger and revenge over the subsequent years that thousands of people went on to lose their lives, either opposing it, defending it or innocently getting caught in between the two. Without it or if by chance I had found myself growing up on the other side of that border, I may not have gone on to experience the major life tragedies that I describe in this book.

Anyway, by no choice of my own, I came into this world in that place, at that time and my parents christened me Patrick Michael McCrystal in Beragh Catholic Church. I am told I was named after my father's brother, Patrick and his uncle Mick and as I was extremely fond of both men in my childhood, I proudly bore my name. My Uncle Patrick and his wife Sarah owned a flax mill at Drumnakilly and they had no children of their own. My bachelor uncle, James, lived with them and ran a tiny shop nearby, selling all sorts of necessities. Their house was a very welcoming place for us children because Patrick was a great storyteller and Sarah was kindly. If Patrick was in the mood for a story everyone would just stop, sit down and gladly listen to his spellbinding tales. He had a hole in one of his ear lobes, the shape of a diamond and I always wondered why, but I never got a straight answer from him about it until many years later. My sister, Mary Elizabeth, was called Lizzie most of the time at home and Mary at school. Well, Lizzie and I could sit around under Uncle Patrick's feet all day and listen to the stories he told the farmers as the carts of flax rolled in from the countryside to be scutched into linen at his mill. He had stories of far-away places and historical characters, of battles and knights and wayfaring strangers. Everyone marveled at his vivid imagination, about the little details of things he had never even seen, heard or tasted. The local people coming into the mill and the shop to pick up the essentials from James also had wonderful news to tell in return and we were all young ears as we listened to the local gossip. Lizzie and I learned all about life and human behaviour right there at the mill. The shop was very small, yet packed full of all sorts of useful things for the home and the farm. It was a real general store, with sweets in glass jars and all. Uncle James didn't have a reputation for giving away free sweets or anything, as he was not the most pleasant of creatures, but Lizzie and I were eternally optimist about the possibly of getting a sweet or two some day. No, we didn't go to Drumnakilly to see Uncle James, but to get good quality attention from Uncle Patrick and Aunt Sarah.

The linen industry was big business in Northern Ireland in those days and our area of Tyrone was a great flax-growing centre. Linen making was traditional in Ireland since the twelfth century, being a huge export commodity for the country. The flax was grown and scutched locally and then sent to the factories in the east of the province to weave into linen cloth. The flaxseed was traditionally sown around St. Patrick's Day in March and harvested in the weeks following the 12th July. This was ideal timing for fitting around the other farming events of the year, such as hay and turf cutting in early summer and the autumn potato harvesting. The flax flower is either blue or white, and I remember the beautiful sight of all the blooming flax fields around the Beragh countryside. Nowadays there are no flax fields anywhere to be seen on the Tyrone landscape and the mills are gone from the riverbanks. But flax will always be part of our Ulster heritage, so much so that the flax flower went on to form the emblem of the new Northern Ireland Government Assembly in the 21st Century.

As children in the 1920's, Lizzie and I watched as the flax crop was pulled by hand in the summer. It was not cut, as cutting would leave the fibres too short. The farmer then retted, or softened the flax by partially rotting it, by immersing the crop in still water dams or lint dams for six to eight weeks. This was labour intensive work and wading through the smelly water was unpleasant. As the flax rotted, we could smell its vile odor as we walked past the lint dams that farmers had built all over the countryside. The flax was then lifted out of the dams and laid out in the fields again to dry. Once dried, the crop was then loaded onto carts and taken to a scutch mill like my uncle's. Scutching is the process of extracting linen fibres from flax stems. The work in the scutch mill was a highly dangerous occupation, as scutchers were at risk from fast moving powerful machinery. Uncle Patrick's mill was sited on the banks of a small river at Drumnakilly, which generated enough force to turn the wheel and drive the machinery. Mill owners were generally farmers who supplemented their income by owning a mill. They usually waited until the outside work was completed for the year and then retreated to the indoor work of milling on the short, dark and cold days of late autumn and winter. Inside the mill, the air was thick with dust and there was a great risk of fire. Uncle Patrick would firstly pass the crop through cogged rollers to break up the outer layer and the woody core. He would then hold the bundle of flax stems into the path of spinning blades to remove any non-fibre material. The process was later repeated with the blades at a finer setting until all the unwanted material was removed and only a bundle of flax fibres remained. Many times we sat at a distance and watched our aunt and uncle work through bundle after bundle of flax as they converted it to silky strands of linen fibre. We were well warned to stay away from the dangerous machinery, but observing was allowed.

My Dad's only sister, auntie Mary-Ann was married to Frank Maguire and they also owned a flax mill. It was possibly one the first oil-driven mills in the country and did not rely on the river for power. The Maguires had ten children and they were our only cousins on the McCrystal side of the family. They were all a little older than us, so we did not play with them often, except at Uncle Mick's house or at school. Uncle Mick was really our grandfather's brother and all the cousins loved playing up at his house as Mick was good to us and we could walk around after him without ever being chased. He gave us bread and jam when we called with him after school. Like granda, he was a farmer, but also worked at a corn mill. In fact all the McCrystals were millers, except for my father, Thomas who worked with horses. He worked at the local farms, training and tending the valuable equine farm stock, as in those days; horses were used for most transporting and farm work. Our family moved around a lot with his career, as daddy was allocated a cottage to live in, with each new farm job, although we never ventured very far from the village of Beragh.

All the McCrystal family had been quiet, hard working people, with little time for dreaming about an ideal world or politics. Granny McCrystal was a cool and austere woman, devoted to hard work and I avoided her like the plague. In fact, I only remember meeting her on a number of occasions, as Granda James usually came to visit us on his own. One time she gave Lizzie and me tea in a bowl instead of a cup and we refused to drink it. Granny believed in wasting nothing and she was very cross with us. I don't remember much else about her and she died young. On the other hand, Granda James was very much part of our lives, as he played cards in our house. He had a crimson red handkerchief in his breast pocket and highly polished shoes, as reflective as mirrors. We children could look at ourselves in granda's shoes as we rolled about the floor, while the adults played games of whist with the cards. Our aunt, Mary-Ann Maguire was strict like her mother before her and she also died young when she went to nurse some of her grandchildren with diphtheria and caught it herself. Some of the Maguire grandchildren died at that time as well.

In contrast, my mother was lighthearted and jolly. Her name had been Susan McGinn before she married my father. Dad's first wife, Mary had died young of tuberculosis, leaving us with two older stepsisters Annie and Gertrude and one stepbrother Anthony. They did not live with us, as Dad had promised their mother to leave them in the care of their maternal grandmother, Granny O'Neill, as Gertie was only three years old at the time and Dad needed to work to feed them. So when Dad married my mother, he set up a new home with us, but faithfully dressed up on a Sunday and headed off to see his other family and we sometimes went along with him. We liked going to Granny O'Neill's, as she had a great big fire and something nice for us to eat on Sundays. My sister Mary Elizabeth was a year older than me and we were the oldest of eleven children in our family. The two children born after me, Margaret and then Thomas died in early childhood leaving a five-year gap between my next brother, Peter, and me.

My father, Thomas, had a total of sixteen children born to him, yet Lizzie and I were like our own separate family because of the age gaps. Two of his first family had died in infancy and then the two in our family also. Additional to this grief, I can remember the distress at home when I was about seven, at the death of our younger brother Francis and our only other sister Veronica Grace. They had eaten pears from a bucket outside a shop, which must have been contaminated and both of them became very ill. They were both taken to the Tyrone County Hospital in Omagh where one died at six o'clock in the evening and the other around midnight. I often wonder how my mother coped with the tragic loss of four children, but at the time I was too young to understand the full impact. Lizzie and I simply availed of the freedom to run and play to avoid the pain in the house. Our therapy became the beautiful countryside around us as we played the pain away.

It is easier now for me to understand why my father was a man with so little to say. I reckon he had suffered so much loss in his young life and he had no ability to express his grief. Like most Irish people, he only had music and literature to give a voice to his feelings. Lizzie and I still recall daddy having a gramophone at home, with one particular song that he frequently played called the Lament of the Irish Emigrant. Written by Lady Helen Selina Blackwood, an Englishwomen who later became the Countess of Gifford, the song portrayed a great understanding of the Irish situation during the famine of the 1840's by a lady who by birth and title, could have chosen never to see the real world outside her window. Very few English landlords attempted to assist the starving poor on their lands during the famine, but some did. Of course as a boy, the significance of the words to my father's situation didn't strike me, but my sister was aware and still thinks this song must have been difficult for our mother to hear and accept as daddy's grief for his first wife.

Lament of the Irish Emigrant.

I'm sittin' on the stile, Mary,
Where we sat side by side
On a bright May mornin' long ago
When first you were my bride;
The corn was springin' fresh and green,
And the lark sang loud and high—
And the red was on your lip, Mary,
And the love-light in your eye.

'Tis but a step down yonder lane,
And the little church stands near,
The church where we were wed, Mary,
I see the spire from here.
But the graveyard lies between, Mary,
And my step might break your rest—
For I've laid you, darling! down to sleep,
With your baby on your breast.

I thank you for the patient smile
When your heart was fit to break,
When the hunger pain was gnawin' there,
And you hid it, for my sake!
I bless you for the pleasant word,
When your heart was sad and sore—
O, I'm thankful you are gone, Mary,
Where grief can't reach you more!

Hearing the lyrics now, I can understand the meaning my sister interpreted from the words, but mammy didn't seem annoyed to me and she sang along with all the records. She was a great singer and loved to sing around the house and at family gatherings. Our house was a great place for a ceili at night, with neighbours gathering in for the evening around the fire as the sound of stories and songs drifted from the little cottage. That specific lament was about the loss of life during the famine years in Ireland, particularly between 1845 and 1850, when the population of Ireland dropped from approximately eight million to under five million people due to starvation or emigration over that period. My grandparents had lived through these times and I suppose the memory and fear of hunger, mass death and abandonment had not yet evolved out of the Irish psyche, leaving many of our people broken and harsh.

Songs, poems and storytelling are such a great tradition of Irish life, that the words were vitally important and children had to learn every word and the history associated with the songs. The story of our history was passed down, from generation to generation, sitting around the fire. The stories at night still told of horrific scenes of evictions and of walking skeletons begging for food. There was one particular story that fascinated me about the famine, which told of the only people who sent help to Ireland; an Ottoman Sultan from Turkey, the poor people of the city of Calcutta in India and a group of American Choctaws Indians, all people who understood famine because of their own histories. What generous people they were to take an interest in the plight of our nation, at a time when communication was so limited and even our close neighbours had ignored our plight. I wonder if I was drawn to those stories because my soul subconsciously knew that hunger and the aid of others would be a major issue in my future life.

There were also stories of the dreaded workhouse, were families had been separated from each other and no-one ever wanted to go there. Also the stories of the lucky local families who had escaped to make a new life in America were popular. People in our area were always dreaming of a good life in America. The family of James Buchannan Jr., a former United States President, had emigrated from their Irish home beside us in Brackey. My mother's family were delighted that her cousin, Fr.

Edward McGinn became Bishop of Albany, New York and there is still a High School named after him there. But, not all stories of emigration were so romantic, because thousands of people had died on the coffin ships to Canada and America and many others had been shipped to Australia as convicts for stealing food during those harsh famine years in Ireland. The cities of England and Scotland overflowed with the sheer numbers of Irish families who arrived begging for food.

The Great Famine in Ireland certainly influenced Irish thinking and I suppose eventually motivated the push for independence. Although we heard the songs and stories of rebellion and suppression in our house, they did not incite us to anger, as I believe my parents had experienced enough sorrow of their own without looking to create more bother. My grandparents showed little sign of emotion about such things either and Daddy worked hard and was away from home a lot. He had no emotive ideas about politics or stories of injustices. In fact, Daddy never told us much about anything I suppose, but he was good enough and very particular about good manners and thanking people.

On the other hand, our mother was the centre of our world. Despite all her tragedy, Mammy was always positive and our home was a happy welcoming place with stories of leprechauns and fairies and the land of Tir Na nOg. This was a mythical place of eternal youth and happiness, in the western isles of our dreams. The neighbours always called on Mammy for a visit and before long the singing would start and the night would roll in fast, as we children finally fell asleep to the sound of Mammy's voice. I was not a singer like my brother Peter, but I loved to sit and listen to the stories and the songs. Our house was full of laughter, with jokes, funny stories and good neighbours, and Mammy always said: "The party is never over until 'Danny Boy' has been sung."

Living in the country gave my sister and me great freedom. Of course we had some jobs to do around home, but we were not exploited. At home we always had a cow for milk, hens and ducks for eggs and an occasional chicken for dinner. We had vegetables and potatoes growing and Mammy always reared turkeys to sell at Christmas. We did not own the farm, but we were lucky to have rented use of it to grow some food. Along with helping Mammy with the household chores, we children also helped save the hay and turf in summer and plant and gather the potato crop in spring and autumn. We made as much fun as we could out of these seasonal events. Granted the work was labour intensive, but we loved those days. For me, the best time was during the corn harvest when the children had to prop up the sheaves of corn in groups of four called a stook. The lads always had a race to get the most work done before the rain would come. The crop was left like this in the field to dry before we built them into rucks or stacks on top of a bed of whin's or gorse bush to elevate them off the wet ground. Later the corn was brought to Granda's work place at the mill for threshing. We had a donkey and cart for that sort of work.

The rest of our childhood was spent going to school and playing. Lizzie and I ran through fields playing hide and seek and keeping busy. I remember making Easter huts and searching for stray eggs for boiling in the hut. We loved the springtime of year, as we gathered flowers, barefoot in the meadow, to place on our May altar. May is the month of the Virgin Mary, and in Ireland an altar was made in each house to honour her. We loved mud and both of us could easily spend our time making mud pies or plastering the mud up against old walls for fun. Sometimes we went to school in the village and other times we went to the country school in Brackey, depending on what farm daddy was employed with at the time.

PACKIE AND LIZZIE AT SCHOOL 1929

At the school in Beragh village, the boys played football at breaktime and then on the way home again. The game was played with a very small, hard ball called a handball, as we did not have access to a real football. The match was played up and down the village street in a highly competitive fashion, with very ambiguous rules. It was neither Soccer nor Gaelic football and it often ended as a wrestling match. Beragh had just one long wide street, with a mixture of residential and commercial premises running along each side. You have to remember there was very little traffic then, except for an odd horse and cart travelling through town at a trot or slower, so the street was as good as a football pitch to us lads. I only remember one motorcar in Beragh at that time, belonging to Conways in the draper shop. When it first arrived in town one lad had a good look around the car and said to Mr. Conway "do you see when this thing has pups, could you keep me one please".

We walked to Brackey School across the fields and over the footbridge across the river. My grandfather worked at the corn mill beside the footbridge, providing us with a warm fire to huddle at in winter on our way to and from school. Old granda James never had much to say, but he never chased us from the fire. He was a very tidy man, who dressed well and kept his shoes in high shine, sporting a red handkerchief neatly folded in his breast pocket for social occasions. Even though he worked in a dusty old mill, he always wiped the dust off his seat before sitting down anywhere and I suppose I could say he had some style about him, but I have no idea where he got the motto of, "being poor is no excuse for poor manners". My father inherited that attitude, as he was a stickler for decorum and doing a thing properly.

In spring and summer we shed our shoes and went barefoot through the tall, soft grass and we often waded in the river. We loved the summer months, with so much freedom to be outside. Autumn was another favourite season for finding apples, plums and berries, but of course the chestnuts were the most important treasure, as they were desperately needed for playing conkers. There was a huge competition every year to find the biggest, strongest conker and have it triumph over all other chestnuts. The game was taken very seriously and kept us children busy searching and playing for weeks. The winter was mostly a miserable time of year, with long dark nights and cold wet days. This was the time for visiting neighbours and sitting together around the fire to tell stories and sing songs to keep the spirits high. I remember getting wet nearly every day going and coming from school and on the weekly two mile walk to Mass on a Sunday. We would sit through the service in our wet clothes and then walk two miles home again. No wonder people died young from all sorts of illness.

Our Lizzie was very smart at her schoolwork and I remember the headmaster begging my parents to send her to secondary school in the town. But Omagh was over six miles away which was an impossible distant without transport. We probably didn't have the money for books and uniforms and certainly not for boarding, so Lizzie missed out and went away to work in a house about ten miles from home instead. I was average at school and not really too interested in study. There weren't any jobs about to motivate a boy to study anyway. I was full of devilment as a lad, climbing trees for apples or hiding people's bicycles or wheelbarrows. I loved Halloween, when all the lads could remove farm gates and hide them, or we would tie a fine thread to the doorknockers in the village and pull them from around the corner. If only Halloween could have last all year round. Luckily, I was a fast runner and never got caught unless someone told my daddy. There is an old saying in our country, "If you see a lad on the road give him a clip on the ear, as he is either coming from or going to trouble." That was definitely true of me until I was a teenager and then I settled down. We could not afford to send me any further up the academic ladder either, but my parents kept me at Primary School for as long as possible. Anyway I was far too energetic to be wasting time sitting in a classroom and I was glad to say goodbye when I finally left.

Chapter Five

A TOUGH DECISION

I think I left school when I was about fourteen and then drifted from odd job to odd job until I was seventeen. All the young men were looking for the same jobs and everyone had to fight for a chance of a day's pay. The economic problems began in 1929 with the worldwide recession following the Wall Street Crash. The Belfast shipbuilder Harland & Wolff was in decline even though they had once been the largest shipyard in the world and had built the "Titanic". The linen industry was facing competition from new synthetic fabrics so my uncle's flax mill business started to suffer and certainly could not afford to employ me. The number of unemployed rose steadily in Northern Ireland and in 1932 there were over 70,000 out of work in the wee North. Things were even worse in the Free State and England, so emigration there was pointless, though some families did head for America from our rural area during this time.

Ireland was not the only country with troubles. The effect of the Great Depression was also unsettling the rest of Europe, especially the German economy, which was already crippled by the demands of the Treaty of Versailles, signed at the end of World War One. The Treaty ended the war between Germany and the Allied powers, but it was not an agreed peace treaty and was more of a crushing economic revenge against Germany which left its people suffering and angry. Nonetheless, it was signed on 28 June 1919, just after I was born and fueled the rise of Nazism in Germany during the early years of my life. The War may have toppled the Imperialist rule of the Russian, German, Ottoman and the Austro-Hungarian Empires, but it replaced them with an equally oppressive Fascist or Communist rule in those countries. It was the same old story of the poor paying the price for the power struggle of the elite few. As the economic crisis of the 1930's blackened, Germany, Italy, Russia and Japan began dreaming of expanding their borders and avenging the wrongs of the past through invasion of their neighbouring countries and in many cases with a policy of ethnic cleansing and genocide.

By 1936 I was a seventeen-year-old lad, still at home with my parents in a small cottage in Tyrone. I knew nothing of world politics and I did not remember the Great War, later called the First World War. My uncle Patrick said it was called, "the war to end all wars," and rightly so. He never said why he thought that. My mother was expecting her tenth child, Lizzie had moved away to find work and the rest of my brothers were still at school. Without Lizzie, my mother must have felt isolated, with few other women folk of her family around. Her father had been a shoemaker in Beragh but he had died before she had any memory of him. Mammy's sister Maggie lived in Belfast, so it was her other sister, Mary Mulholland who came to our house to help with the babies as they were born. Mammy was not always in the best of health and she was glad to have me around to help with the household chores. I suppose I learned a lot about running a house at this time.

I was Mammy's blue-eyed boy and we were very close. She needed me about, but the reality was about making ends meet. I was another grown-up mouth to feed and I couldn't find enough work to regularly contribute to the household. Teenagers need to feel useful and I was desperately searching for a sense of purpose. I was no different from all the lads around me. Some of my schoolmates got their fulfillment as volunteers in the underground IRA (Irish Republican Army), with aims of driving the British out of Ireland. These lads gained a great thrill, but they brought no money home to their mothers and there was a high risk of imprisonment or injury and my mother needed no more tragedy. Naturally passion runs through the veins of young people and they want to change the world and make things right, but I wasn't sure that this was the way to go about it.

Northern Ireland was a newly formed occupied state, only born fifteen years earlier from a bloody civil war and the nationalist youth did not know where they belonged. Of course the elders on all sides had debts of revenge to settle and all they needed to do was harness the passion of the youth, youths who had no work or outlet for expression. Some families admired martyrdom for their country and these boys had little decision to make, but my parents never instilled any hatred or idealism in my heart. I was free to be confused about which path to take. For peaceful folks like my parents any sort of army career was not considered acceptable, but I needed to be my own man and contribute some way. Obviously other lads struggled to make these same choices between cultural honour and practical survival, as I remember one family nearby who had one son join the British Army and his brother join the IRA. Both those lads died in their early twenties, in the line of duty and fighting for freedom; one in France and the other nearer home. At the end of the day war is war and all sides suffer.

Poverty and the passion of youth make a wonderful breeding ground from where the warlords could select their foot soldiers. In every war the warlords play their games for wealth, power or glory and the poor get their sons returned home dead or injured. But we young lads at that time had no memory or understanding of the horrors of war-we just wanted money and to feel important. The British Army offered work and training when Ireland could offer us nothing. I was intelligent enough to do the math and simply go for the best offer; after all, Irishmen had been fighting in foreign armies for centuries, often for a living and sometimes for a strongly held belief. It is estimated that 350,000 Irishmen served in the British Army during the

First World War. The Irish fought in nearly every European battle throughout history and on both sides of the American civil war. In 1936 many Irish lads including IRA soldiers went off to Spain to fight in the Spanish Civil War, some as Fascists and some as opposing Socialists. That choice did not make them any less Irish or suddenly transform them into Spanish or Americans, as they all either survived or died as Irishmen, no matter which army they served under. Intelligence is credited as being the ability to adapt to change and survive, even if the pill is bitter to swallow. Survival during hard times is easier if you don't bite off the hand that feeds you or cut off your nose to spite your face and the army was a chance at survival.

Now in my nineties, I can look back over a lifetime and see numerous points in my life when my path arrived at a crossroads. As I stood at each junction, a decision had to be made about which direction to take. With the benefit of hindsight, it is easy to call a decision a mistake or credit it as a good choice, but the wisdom of hindsight is not there to help when the dilemma is demanding an answer. At the tender age of seventeen, I was presented with my first life-changing decision to make. Each path in front of me led in completely differing directions and none of them offered a crock of gold at the end of the rainbow, but I had to choose one.

It sounds very glamorous to say that I decided to join the British Army to see the world and have the opportunity to forge out my own path to independence. That story gives the illusion that I was in complete control of my life. But when seriously considered now in the context of the bleak economic climate of mid-thirties rural Ireland, I realise I had no other option. The reality was a fair choice; to survive or not. Our home was no different from most in our rural area as work was scarce for most people. There was little work in the cities either and reports from England didn't offer much hope, and I couldn't afford the train and boat fares to get there anyway. Many of my peers had joined the Army and when they came home for a visit, it was exciting to hear the reports about the good life. The food was good with four meals a day, there was a bed of your own and new boots and a uniform. Compared to our home accommodation, this sounded like a hotel. The wage was five bob or should I say, five shillings a week. A further five bob was paid directly to your parents. The term 'bob' is not commonly used now, but is still used to indicate 5 pence. The 5 pence coin is the same size and weight, and has the same value, as the old shilling coin. So I was paid '5 bob' or 25 pence. It was no fortune anyway, but better than nothing.

The garrison town of Omagh was six miles away from my home and I had rarely visited there in my childhood. As the county town, it was a busy place with government buildings and two hospitals, and the British Army had maintained a training base there since 1875 so Omagh residents were well accustomed to seeing soldiers around the streets. Following the partition of the country in 1922, the camp became a strategic base for the maintenance of the border with the Free State; which was less than 20 miles away at its closest point. In fact, the base was a great economic benefit to the town and remained so until its closure in 2007.

It was not a popular option for a Catholic to join the British army in those days, or at anytime since, but many of us northern Catholics did it at that time anyway, as did over a hundred thousand Irish lads from the Irish Free State. Recession is a mild word to use for the hard times experienced in Ireland during the 1930's, so thinking it my best option, I made the unpopular decision to follow many of my generation and join up. It is easier to make popular decisions in a healthy economic climate. My mother was distraught, and, listening to my sister now, I appreciate the pain she suffered at letting me go, but she had no alternative to offer me and she had no more choice than I had.

As I look around me now, at the modern 21st century, I wonder if the current seventeen year olds understand the value of the freedom they have to make real choices. I realise their generation faces different challenges and maybe in some ways their choices are becoming more limited again, since the turn of the millennium and the downturn in the economy. But hopefully they will always live in a free society, offering them the potential to create their own future. These opportunities were unheard of in my youth.

Chapter Six

ARMY ADVENTURES

Just after Christmas, in early January 1937, at the age of seventeen and a half, I hitched a lift to Omagh and walked into St. Lucia's barracks. I had convinced myself that I wanted to see the world and my family needed the five bob a week. Moving into Omagh would be an adventure and I was joining lads my own age. I had one little problem in that I needed to be eighteen to join so luckily with either a slip of my tongue or the slip of the recruiting officer's pen, the year of my birth became 1918. I signed my name to serve for seven years active duty and a further five on reserve, called a 7 n' 5. The numbers meant little to me as I had no concept of time, and it was great to finally have a real job.

The training started right away and although the exercises were strange at first, we country lads knew all about hard work and we were already in good shape and well able to keep up with the strenuous schedule. The mornings started early with a call to the square to practice drills and then physical training, or as we called it PT, in the gym. We were often sent on a four-mile run before breakfast. It was safe for uniformed soldiers to go outside the barracks in those days, unlike the years during the Troubles from 1969 until the present day. The run route took us up the steep hill of Castle Street, to the chapel, where we turned into

James Street, all the way out the Tamlaght Road and back into town along the Brookmount Road. We were always well ready for breakfast by the time we arrived back. That meal consisted of a fried egg, bread and tea, or sometimes a kipper with tea, bread and marmalade. After breakfast it was back to the square to learn firearm skills and then more drills. There was a break at eleven for a mug of tea or soup, if you were lucky. Dinner was from 1pm to 2pm with a variety of stews or sausages or bacon with potatoes and vegetables. For dessert we often got tinned fruit, bread puddings or cakes, but we always got awful runny custard—well, let us say you couldn't eat it with a fork. We may have complained about the custard then, but in the years to come, I spent many long days and nights fantasising about that custard and how good it might taste.

When you experience starvation, even the memory and precise description of food brings some comfort. The good food I enjoyed during those months in St. Lucia's barracks went on to nourish many a fantasy in later years. To this day my family will tell you that I am very attentive to the details regarding food. No matter what the occasion, I will always remember what we ate. I spent many a long evening attempting to remember exactly what we ate back in Ireland in 1937, therefore I can tell you with confidence that, at teatime from 4pm to 5pm we had a cup of hot tea, bread and jam or cheese the odd time. The late supper was usually more tea and bread with tinned fish. That was four meals a day during the week, but only three at the weekends so we thought we felt hungry on Saturday and Sunday. On top of all those breaks to eat, we rested for ten minutes every hour for a smoke. I didn't smoke, but I didn't miss out on the rest.

Boy, my life had changed completely from my world on the farm in the country, and although I secretly missed my family, I was delighted with the new conversations and the opportunities to learn new and interesting skills. I was taught the proper way to care for my belongings and myself and now I could shine boots as good as my grandfather. We were confined to barracks for the first six weeks of training before getting a few hours freedom to go into town on a Saturday evening. When I did get out, I just walked up and down the main street of Omagh as I had no money or any idea what to do in a town. Home was six miles away, so I did not have the time to get there and back, as we had to return to the barracks by 11.59 pm sharp. When the wages finally arrived, I had five bob per week. With that I had to buy a cleaning kit, with special polish for my boots and Brasso and a chamois for polishing my buttons and such. With the little I had left, I treated myself to a plate of chips at the Naffi canteen on the Saturday night. I can tell you the money was light. At least my Mum got the other five bob and she had to make it stretch even further.

Every Sunday morning we were marched up the hill, behind the army band to the top of Castle Street. We Catholics went into the Sacred Heart Church for Mass and the others went to their religious gathering. Most of the churches in Omagh are sited there at the top of the hill. The Church of Ireland, The Methodist, the Presbyterian and the Catholic churches all sat comfortably together in harmony. Any other lads who didn't want to go to church had to stand to attention outside the churches for the duration. It was much easier to attend a service.

St Lucia's in Omagh had been the barracks for the Royal Inniskilling Fusiliers, up until Partition in 1922, when the Inniskilling or Skins, as they were nicknamed were disbanded and then formed a two-battalion corps with the Royal Irish Fusiliers, sharing the Omagh depot. With the independence of the Irish Free State, all the Irish regiments down south were disbanded, but in 1937 there was an expansion of the British army and the Inniskilling came to life again when the Battalion was revived at Omagh and a 2nd Battalion of the Royal Irish Fusiliers was also reformed there. I joined up just as these changes occurred and, although I served in the 2nd Battalion of Royal Irish Fusiliers, I had a Skins Army Number 6978489. Our main barracks was in Armagh and they traditionally recruited from the counties of Armagh, Cavan and Monaghan, while the Skins came from Tyrone, Fermanagh, Donegal and Derry. But since Partition, our ranks also contained many lads from all over Ireland who came north looking to join under an Irish-named regiment. One lad from Dublin told me his mother sent him to join a regiment with Irish in the name.

The Royal Irish Fusiliers had a long history of serving in wars all over the world such as the Crimean and Boer wars. During the Napoleonic wars, at the battle of Barrosa on the 5th March, in 1812, the Irish Fusiliers were the first British battalion to capture a French Imperial Eagle in battle, thus earning an eagle for the Regimental Coat of Arms, along with a harp and shamrocks. Every year on the 5th March the officers had to serve us soldiers our breakfast in celebration of this day and we really enjoyed that. It was during the Peninsular War that the regiment got its nickname, the Faughs, (the fogs) because of the Irish language battle cry, "Faugh À Ballagh", used by the fusiliers meaning, "Clear the Way". During the First World War they served at the Somme and the Dardanelles and therefore the regiment had a reputation as tough and experienced and we were expected to keep up the good name.

As the months of 1937 rolled in, the training became very strict as we were preparing for the Coronation of King George VI following the abdication of his older brother Edward. All the drills had to be done in silence, with no spoken commands. The orders were given by hand signals, so we had to pay extra special attention. I gave my full attention to the commands as I didn't want to miss an action and get roared at by the sergeant or laughed at later by my mates. The Bara or Barrosa 500 Squad consisted of lads all over six foot tall and I so wanted to be in that squad, but I was only five foot eight inches. They got the honour of going to London to march in the Coronation Parade in May. Afterwards, they were invited to St. James' Palace and presented with the colours of the Second Battalion of the Royal Irish Fusiliers. The Baras also got to wear a special uniform made of blue-dyed, Khaki and I was left to watch on, wishing I could have been tall like my father.

In June, we were freed for a few days of holidays, before our move to England. At long last, I got home to my family in Beragh, even though it was to say goodbye. There was a gathering in the house, but it was more like a wake than a leaving party. Mammy usually loved a house party, but there was no singing those few days. I didn't understand what all the fuss was about anyway and I remember my brothers were more interested in my uniform, which I thought was cool. Nobody told me what was wrong and was too excited to ask. I suppose I was only a child in many ways, but I was learning a thing or two about looking after myself from the town boys at the barracks.

So two weeks after the Coronation in June 1937, I said my goodbyes, packed up my meagre belongings and climbed onto the train in Omagh with my new mates, destined for the first big adventure of my life. I was so excited to get on the train and see the city of Belfast. I did not realise the world was so huge. We embarked on the boat to England and found ourselves in Borden Camp, Hampshire. It was a huge army camp for more advanced combat training and we spent about six to eight weeks there before a further move to the Corona Barracks in Aldershot. It was here I met Walter Pancott, a lad from Omagh, who had been in the army a year or so ahead of me, so he knew his way about and kept us new Omagh recruits on the right track amongst thousands of lads from all over Britain, Ireland and many other countries of the Commonwealth. I was sharp enough and learned the social and military skills quickly, thus avoiding any hassle. I was also a good runner and athlete, a positive attribute in the army and also we country boys were as strong as oxen, which kept most bullies at a distance. We spent our days at fitness training and learning about combat, with lessons on firearms, big guns and survival skills. This was our home for the next six months, bringing it up to Christmas.

The Irish lads had become good friends, regardless of our religious or cultural differences and I suppose we were like a family of sorts, as we grew accustomed to life away from home. First names were not used in the army, just a nickname along with your surname, such a Spud Murphy, Skin Kelly, Nagger Hackett, Larky McManus or Smugger Smith and Chalky White. If a man was tall he was Lofty, small he was Titch, the Scottish were Jock, the Welsh Taffy and the Londoners were Tosh. I was simply P or McCrystal as there was no one else with the McCrystal name in the Battalion. We learned all the abbreviations and army slang words and by the time we were on the boat home to Ireland for the Christmas holidays, the country boys had turned into cool dudes. We talked of our next great adventure to Malta in the New Year and our social plans for the holidays at home.

It was great to see everyone at home and tell them of my travels and the sights I had seen in England. But soon I reverted back to being a country boy again, among my own community and settled in to the comfort of a traditional Irish family Christmas. We may not have had much, but we certainly could make a party out of very little and Mum was not as morbid this time, as she sang and cooked with delight at having both Lizzie and me home. Therefore, I did not make a big deal about my future trip to Europe and nobody seemed that interested anyway. Only Uncle Patrick showed an understanding about the adventure of a trip to the Mediterranean. He seemed to have read a lot about the world, as he told me some great historical tales of Europe and he wished me well. I spent some time with Uncle Mick over Christmas as well and I helped him feed the animals and discuss the more local issues of Beragh. Lizzie made me curl her hair with a hot iron before we went to the dance and whispered something about Gertie not being well. I stayed two weeks at home with my family over Christmas and as much as I enjoyed the time, I was happy enough to return to my army life with my mates. Daddy had been his normal quiet self, but I do believe he had a tear in his eye, when he hugged me goodbye saying "You be home soon son." If I'd known that day how long I was to be exiled from Beragh and all that I loved, the embraces of farewell might have been tighter.

I remember the day we returned to England, as the lads all met up at the Central Bar in Omagh. I wasn't taking a drink at that time as I was too young, but I was delighted to see everyone again and we had lots of stories to tell about dances we had attended during the holidays. We all boarded the mail train to Belfast at 5pm and then stepped onto what we called the Cattle Boat to Liverpool. The boat was full of cows who; along with us spent the night rolling about on the Irish Sea waves in a gale-force storm. I lay on the broad of my back to prevent getting sea-sickness and I remember the noise of the wind, people being sick and those cows roaring all night. We were not looking forward to the longer cruise to Malta. I really believe I had no idea were Malta was or how far away it was from home, but I knew it was going to take seven days on the sea.

PACKIE AT SEVENTEEN

Chapter Seven

A YOUTH IN MALTA

Just as the New Year commenced in January 1938, I was in Southampton on the southern coast of England and about to step on to a huge luxury ocean liner called the SS California, bound for the biggest adventure of my life. There was no way of knowing that eight years would pass before I was to see home again; my only interest at that moment was in the enormous vessel towering above me in the harbour. It was bigger than the length and breath of Beragh village I thought. Our Regimental band played "Auld Lang Syne" as we pulled away from the dock. "Should old acquaintance be forgot, and never brought to mind? Should old acquaintance be forgot, for auld lang syne?" The ship was beautiful with chandeliers and fancy furniture, things I had never seen the like of before in my life. The SS California was famous for being the closest ship to the Titanic the night it sunk. But a German U-boat had sunk that SS California during the First World War and this replacement ship had been built in 1923 in Glasgow. It had three funnels, with only the middle one working. The ship was still in use as a luxury cruise liner, but the Admiralty must have hired it to bring us troops to Malta.

On board, life was much the same as on land except for the luxurious surroundings. We spent the days cleaning up or peeling potatoes, cleaning toilets or scrubbing the decks. We continued training with drills, square-bashing and keeping fit by running around the full length of the ship. The sailing was extremely smooth, especially after we cleared the Bay of Biscay and the weather grew noticeably warmer as we sailed through the Straits of Gibraltar and into the Mediterranean Sea. I listened attentively to every detail I could hear from the crew or our officers, so I could picture our progress on a map. Even at that young age, I loved talking to people and learning from them. I had always paid great attention to detail and finally my mind was getting real nourishment. The journey lasted about seven days and I remember the awesome views and beautiful climate as we neared a strange new land. Malta was just a small dot on the horizon at first, but as the ship approached the coast, I was astounded by the colossal stone fortifications surrounding the magnificent harbour, later to be known to us as Grand Harbour.

The capital city of Valletta was built on a high-ridged peninsula, sticking out to sea like a long finger. Its towering walls rose high above the two natural deepwater harbours, which flanked the city on both sides. The headlands on the opposite shores wrapped protectively around the harbours giving the ultimate protection, with magnificent forts strategically positioned at the point of each jut of land. The Knights of St John built the city in the 16th century as a fortress to protect from invaders, especially the Turks who were greatly feared. Uncle Patrick had told me that the mighty Turkish Ottoman Empire had ruled the Mediterranean and beyond for centuries, but Malta had kept them out. The British had suffered heavy losses at the Battle of Gallipoli (The Dardanelles) against the Turks during the First World War and the Ottoman Empire only collapsed after that war. I also remembered that an Ottoman Sultan had sent money and ships of food to the Irish during the famine, so I thought they couldn't be all that bad. So here I was, Wee Packie, all the way from Beragh, sailing into a harbour of history. I could never have imagined a scene like this in my wildest dreams. The sea glistened and the surrounding limestone walls emitted a soft, warm glow in the powerful sunlight. It looked like the peninsulas' formed two gentle arms to reach out in a welcoming embrace.

The local people came out to greet us in beautiful coloured fishing boats in an attempt to sell their local produce. Looking down from the deck of our ship I could see boats crammed with fruit, vegetables and wine. Women held up lace and glass ornaments for sale and my head swam with excitement. I could never explain this place to people back home as they would have said I was talking nonsense. The ship docked in Grand Harbour, next to the city of Valletta, and I thought it was the most beautiful place on earth. As we marched the six miles or so to our new camp, I soaked up the sun, the landscape, the sight of the ancient stone buildings and the decorative horse-drawn buggies. I also caught the timbre of the strange sounding Maltese language, spoken by the friendly locals who had stopped to watch our regiment march across their land behind our impressive regimental pipe band. The countryside looked so exotic and as I gazed at the tall palm trees above my head I nearly fell out of step. I must admit I fell in love with Malta at first sight.

Our new home was Mtarfa Barracks in the centre of this little island. The whole island only measured nine miles wide, by nineteen miles long approximately, with two additional tiny islands called Gozo and Comino lying to the north. Mtarfa was a large military barracks with a hospital, situated on one of the highest ridges on Malta, giving it a great vantage point overlooking most of the island. On the neighbouring ridge sat Rabat and the ancient fortified city of Mdina, with their many churches and monasteries. It was amazing to listen to the pealing and tolling of the bells from all the churches in Mdina drifting across the small green valley between us. Mtarfa's large military hospital had cared for the wounded of the First World War, when Malta had been named the "Nurse of the Mediterranean". Thousands of injured soldiers from the Dardanelles were shipped to Malta for care in the modern, state-of-the-art hospitals there.

From Mtarfa ridge, I could see all the way to the sea on both sides of the island and Ta'Qali airfield ran across the flat land of the central plain directly below me. Beside the airstrip sat the village of Mosta with its magnificent domed church rising high above the houses. The people of Mosta had built the church with their own hands in the early 1800's and it was the third largest dome in Europe. The Maltese had great faith and St. Paul the apostle had been shipwrecked on Malta and converted the island to Christianity as early as 60AD. It was nearly four hundred years later before St. Patrick came preaching Christianity in Ireland.

When we arrived in January the weather was warm, healthy and mild nearly every day. If rain fell, it was only for a very short period at a time. The temperature was generally over 12°C in winter, so it was a welcome change for us to complete our exercises warm and dry. That was the only change to our lifestyle in camp, but a day off on our new island home took on a whole new meaning to us Irish lads. The coastal villages were beautiful, with their colourful fishing boats, called luzzu, and the local passenger boats were called dghajsa. The bow of each boat was decorated with a painted eye called "The Eye of Osiris", which is an ancient Phoenician symbol to offer protection from the dangers of the sea. The boats were painted in brightly coloured horizontal strips of yellow, blue, red and white and they bobbed happily on the gleaming aquamarine water.

The picturesque scenes were further enhanced within the backdrop of the honey-coloured, natural stone landscape. The buildings and fortification walls had been constructed with this same local globerigina or coralline limestone over the centuries. The globerigina was a softer rock and being easier to work with, had been used in most of the structures. The harder, more crystalline, coralline stone had been used on the more important buildings. The coastline was rocky, but the blue seas and cloudless skies softened the harshness of the terrain and the hills were dotted with pretty

MAP OF MALTA 1938

MARCHING IN VALLETTA 1938

villages, each dominated by a church spire or dome. Tomatoes, grapes, lemon and limes grew out in the fields and everything looked so colourful in the brilliant sunlight. Stone walls and large cactus plant hedges marked the fields and the farmers worked hard to irrigate their crops from stone water towers, enabling the growth of an abundance of food. Malta has no rivers, so all the water was pumped up from underground and an ancient Roman viaduct carried the water across the island to the city of Valletta. I thought of my family going to Mass in the cold and the wet, while here I could sit in the sun and find a church on every corner.

On my days off, I would wander around the city of Valletta soaking up the atmosphere of the markets and I especially loved the little squares with people sitting around talking and enjoying the weather. It was wonderful to smell the fresh bread soaked in olive oil and covered with tomatoes, garlic and cheese, a meal the locals ate outside together with a local wine. It was easy to settle down to a life in Malta and I remember nights of drifting to sleep in the barracks to the sound of the church bells drifting from Mdina and our regimental band playing "Oft in the Stilly Night."

Not that I spent many nights in the barracks if I was off duty. Our money went a good bit further in Malta and with my training complete I was on full pay. We had a half-day off on Wednesdays and we usually went to the city that day and every night until the money ran out. We rarely stayed in the quiet villages as all the local young people went out to Valletta in the evenings, or to the nightspots of Sliema. There was a roller skating dance held in Sliema and the music played late into the night. The big stars then were Vera Lynn, Bing Crosby, Ann Shelton and Frank Sinatra and it was vital to get to town to hear the latest hits playing in the bars. I had bought a lightweight cotton civvy outfit for going out at night and it was cool to stand at the long narrow bars, talking with friends and listening to the local animated conversations. The Maltese language is Arabic in sound and very difficult to learn as it has been influenced by so many cultures. As the locals talked, it sounded as if they were arguing, with their hands in constant motion, but it was only friendly discussion and over time I picked up an odd word, even if it was only pub talk. Some nights we went for a meal of sausage and champ and often attended the cinema or the bingo afterwards. Some of the boys hung out in shady areas of town, catching diseases or losing money and maybe ending up in jail. It was easier to stay out of bother by enjoying the music in the pubs and sipping on the local Blue Label ale. I also remember evenings spent at the Horse racing and Polo matches in Marsa, but as we hadn't any money, we contented ourselves to watch through the fence. Like all the other fellas I had to get a tattoo, mine being of a butterfly with Malta 1938 engraved on my left forearm. It was only afterwards that I thought my parents would disapprove.

I enjoyed the social life, but like Cinderella we had to be back in the barracks before twelve. To get home fast, four of us usually took the local taxi of a horse and carriage called a Karrozin, but we called it a Garry. There were very few motorized vehicles about the island in those days that weren't for military purposes, so the Garry was the fastest mode of transport. If we were a minute late the punishment was confinement to barracks for fourteen days. I was only confined twice: once for not reading the duty board correctly and once for damaging my uniform. My mates caused the damage really, while playing a practical joke on me. They put something corrosive in my Brasso tin, thus tarnishing my buttons just before an inspection, so I had to listen to the bells and pipe band every night for two weeks, while my friends ran to town. They paid for that in hidden boots and flat bicycle tyres for weeks and we had great fun in those days with my prankster nature from youth giving me an added advantage.

Our captain, named Connors, died suddenly in April, of old age we thought. I think he was about fifty or so, but to a teenager, that was ancient. At his funeral in the peaceful military graveyard near Ta'Qali airfield, I remember recognising many Irish names on the gravestones around me, all aged between eighteen and twenty-five, who had died between 1914 and 1918. It seemed a long time ago, before I was even born and I did not consider why so many Irish lads had died there. Youth is a wonderful gift and only for its unquestioning naivety, humans would be too frightened to progress.

The lifestyle in Malta was fantastic with days on the beach, where I learned to swim in the shimmering clear Mediterranan waters of St Paul's and Mellieha Bays. In fact, I was assigned to the athletic squad to represent the regiment in competitions as a runner, mainly in the one-mile or 880 races. I was allocated special running shoes and a sports kit and I did win a few medals and cups, but my athletic career was not destined to progress as the world had other plans. Our squad spent many days running on the beach and we swam a mile every morning before breakfast, back and forth across St. Paul's Bay. My hair grew blond, my skin tanned and my mates were happy to keep my company in town at night as the dark-haired Maltese girls thought I was cute. I was shy, but many of my mates found girlfriends on the strength of my blond hair.

Life was as far removed from Beragh as imaginably possible. I learned to drive a jeep and a truck and to man a Bofor anti-aircraft gun and handle the QF 6 and 17 pounder anti-tank guns. Every soldier had to do their duty standing guard at the gate of the Governor's Palace on Kingsway in the centre of Valletta. This was like the guards at Buckingham Palace in London, but without the fluffy hats, thank God. Standing still was difficult in the very hot summer weather, but we moved sides, with a small march every few minutes. I liked this job well enough, as I loved Valletta, with its high narrow streets offering shade all day and the noises of family life drifting from the windows of the homes above. The washing lines stretched above my head and the shops and markets buzzed with wheeling and dealing. Young people poured into town in the evening time, after siesta, and some evenings I was forced to watch the fun from my post and other nights I could join in. On a day off, I would wander around looking at the ancient sights or simply drift along the coast and villages.

I discovered that Malta was steeped in history and influenced by every advancing empire throughout time. It had been impacted by the Neolithic, Phoenician, Greek, Roman and Byzantine cultures, long before the arrival of the medieval Knights of the Order of St. John of Jerusalem (later known as The Knights of Malta). The knights were founded in Jerusalem about the 11th century, as a medical order to provide care for the poor and sick pilgrims visiting the Holy Land. During the First Crusades, they became a Catholic military order, to protect the pilgrims. Following the loss of Christian-held territories in the Holy Land to the Turks, the Order arrived at Malta in 1530AD and established a new city, Valletta, the capital of Malta. The island endured a siege in 1565 as islanders prevented the mighty Turkish army from invading its shores and after four months of bitter hand-to-hand fighting, the Turkish army retreated from Malta. It was an amazing defeat at the hands of the Maltese people and the Knights, aided by the impenetrable fortifications. For over two hundred years, the Knights and the Maltese prospered in peace, until the French invaded in 1798 during the Napoleonic wars and expelled the Knights to Rome. The Maltese people revolted against the French, who had plundered their churches and homes, resulting in a two-year siege until the Maltese asked the British to take the island under their protection in 1800 and help drive the French out.

For such a small island, the people were resourceful and successfully expelled or held off some of the most powerful armies in history whenever they threatened their culture. Other invaders were accepted if they brought work and knowledge to the island and did not interfere with their way of life. Although astute, the Maltese were really nice people and very religious, with a great devotion to Our Lady, symbolized by a church or holy statue at every corner. Malta attempted self-governing from 1921 until 1931 with three political parties of Pro-British, Pro-Italian and the small newly formed Labour Party. In 1930 the Pro-Italian party won the election with the backing of the Church from the Vatican and proposed implementing Italian language and culture. Trouble broke out and the country returned to direct British rule. Under a British Governor, the Maltese culture and language was promoted as the joint official language with English. With the growth of Fascism in Italy during the 1930's the Maltese nation were generally happy under the Union Jack as they knew a lot about survival and making a situation work for them. They also knew how to bide their time and form strong alliances, so

Malta remained within the British Empire until its independence in 1964, but continued to house a large British naval base until 1979 in its magnificent harbours. With patience, tolerance and intelligence the Maltese now hold their own independence as a small nation within the great European Union. As for the Knights of the Order of Malta, they dispersed all over the world, now working with the sick and the needy on five continents. Years later and after returning home, I discovered an Order of Malta Ambulance Corps was in existence in my hometown of Omagh and I was delighted about their historical links with the island I had lived on for so long.

I was happy during these peacetime months in Malta, but I was not to stay there for long. Within a few months, my training was finished and I was ready for active service. We went into Valletta to celebrate and I, like all the other lads went for another tattoo, of a Harp and Shamrock, on my arm and by October 1938, I was boarding a troop ship and heading off to Palestine to serve under General Montgomery as a fully-fledged soldier. Around the same time, Germany took control in Austria, and Japan went to war with China. We sailed into the busy port of Haifa and we found a new city to socialise in at night, with its late night teahouses and buzzing atmosphere, but we soon learned that we were not so safe or welcome in this new land.

Palestine is the Arab name for the strip of land where the Middle East meets the Mediterranean Sea. The Ottoman Turks had ruled this area for centuries, until World War One, when the Allied forces drove them out. In the peace talks that followed the end of the war, Syria and Lebanon were handed over to the French and Palestine was allocated to the British. Britain governed under a League of Nations mandate from 1920, but the native Arab population, who had always lived there, claimed Palestine as their homeland. They had fought with the Allies, against the Turks, during the First World War and had felt confident of gaining their land back once the war was over. But, the same area of land had also been promised, it seems, to the Jews and after 1920, many Jews migrated from the increasing persecution in Europe, to this Promised Land and lived with the Arabs in relative harmony until 1929. But the Jews continued flooding in from Europe believing this Holy Land was rightfully theirs too. In 1935, approximately 62,000 Jews immigrated into Palestine in one year alone and naturally the tension increased.

In August 1929, relations between the Jews and Arabs in Palestine flared, with the death of over two hundred people in Jerusalem and in May 1936, more violence occurred and the British had to restore law and order using military force. The violence continued through 1937 as the Arabs and the Jews became increasingly hostile, and they both blamed the British. This was the situation into which our regiment arrived in 1938. The British limited the number of Jewish arrivals to appease the Arabs, but this made the situation worse as both communities became increasingly angry. The Arabs attacked because of broken promises and because the Jews continued arriving illegally. The Jews attacked because the British had imposed restrictions on the amount of land Jews could buy in Palestine. Our work was to man border posts and checkpoints to keep both sides from attacking each other or our forces. We seemed to be generally protecting the Jews against an Arab revolt, even though the Jewish paramilitary, Haganah or the Irgun, did indiscriminately attack also. This hostile environment was a shock to our innocence and we were in constant danger, although I must say in the Arab villages, the people often gave us tea and were generally friendly as we patrolled their streets.

Those months were spent at general duties on the front line, all over the Holy Land. This landscape was very alien at first and the weather was hot and dry, with oranges and grapes growing in the countryside. Fruit was a rare novelty at home in Ireland and it was usually tinned, but here, exotic fruits were fresh and growing in abundance on trees and vines all around us. Of course, we discretely tried them out when the opportunity arose and what a treat that was for us. During that tour we wore ordinary uniforms, but although it was supposedly a peacetime situation, we still had a difficult time watching for snipers and I faced the harsh reality of combat for the first time as we lost a few men from sniper fire. Their loss had a profound effect on me as I realised the job of a soldier was for real and that people did want to kill us, so I became very attentive to my surroundings and learned to watch my back and assess a situation very carefully before making a move.

It was guerrilla warfare, with mines laid along roads, pipelines and railway lines. They attacked us anywhere and we raided their towns and villages in return, looking for weapons and safe houses. There were curfews and arrests, but mainly in Arab communities. Often it was the innocent children who triggered the mines as they played and we had no idea what the enemy looked like, in among the general population. It was a cowardly style of warfare, in among family homes and communities and it was a huge learning curve for us young men who never imagined that our training would lead us into a civilian theatre of battle. When you're young and in a crowd you just follow orders without questioning the bigger picture and we did not fully understand the situation around us. Otherwise most of that tour of duty was relatively uneventful in Palestine, except for the visit of General Montgomery when I was assigned to the truck convey acting as his protection while he toured around Gaza. As an Irishman from Donegal, Montgomery liked to meet the Irish troops and he gained great respect from all the men. We didn't know then how famous he was to become in the history of the world.

On a day off work, I took the opportunity to visit the biblical village of Bethlehem. Our Welsh army chaplain, Father Anwyl, had organized the trip to see the stable were Jesus was born. The stable was more like a cave, with a chapel built on top and I suppose I really didn't understand the privilege it was to make that trip, but I did pray for my family while I was there and especially for my mother and my new baby brother Gerald, who had arrived in September, the letter from home told me. The Army was not so bad really. I was seeing new places, socializing in cosmopolitan city bars and we lads had become good friends, but I did miss my family a little. In March 1939, the radio announced that Hitler had invaded Czechoslovakia and the Spanish Civil War had ended with Franco's Fascist government in charge. Many Irish men died in that war on both sides of the conflict and now the world had to wait and see how friendly Franco and Hitler had become.

Meanwhile, I spent my nineteenth birthday on Mount Carmel, were Elijah spent some of his life, according to the Bible. I had grown accustomed to the separation from home and we lads were all in the same boat together. I was a soldier now and I had no excuse for complaining. The food was generally fine with Maconochie stew made with meat, vegetables and potatoes and the old faithful corned beef or bully beef was always on offer. I completed my first tour of active duty in Palestine mid-April, just after my birthday, and with another tattoo of a goddess engraved on my arm to commemorate the completion of my time in Palestine 1938-39; I boarded the troop ship back to our base on Malta. The excitement of returning to our paradise island had us all in high spirits as we watched the port at Haifa and its uneasy peace fade on the horizon. Some lads had girlfriends to return to and the rest of us had girlfriends to find, so Valletta here we come.

I was too naïve about life to understand that reports of a looming war with Germany could infringe on my life, when in fact I was sailing towards probably the most strategic lump of rock in the Mediterranean. Malta was the only deepwater harbour, ideally positioned halfway between the Strait of Gibraltar and the Suez Canal and therefore considered vitally important to any army. This central position was a prime location for controlling the shipping lanes to and from the Middle and Far East via the Suez Canal. Malta is approximately 90 km south of Sicily and 290 km east of Tunisia, with the Strait of Gibraltar 1,800 km to the west and Alexandria 1,500 km to the east. But, wherever Malta might have been situated, pre-war it was paradise to us lads and my daily reality was of living in a large army base, in beautiful surroundings, with great weather. It was unimaginable that this beautiful tiny island and its lovely people could attract the wrath of war and I innocently had no idea what war entailed. I was delighted to get back to Valletta with my mates for some fun and get another tattoo,—this time a horseshoe saying good luck—but I didn't realise how much luck I was going to need. So I went about living the usual army life of drills and weapons training, while the summer sunshine kept me warm. I could only imagine how cold and damp it was back home and I was glad I had not remained a farm boy out searching for work every day in the rain. I suppose innocence is bliss and even if I had understood the danger I was in, there was no opportunity to change my circumstances. I was condemned to my fate, as there wasn't an emergency exit from the army.

Chapter Eight

WAR IS DECLARED

When Germany invaded Poland, on the first of September 1939, the world finally recognised that they had a problem on their hands and that all of Europe was at risk. Immediately France and the British Commonwealth considered the options and decided to declare war on Germany two days later. We heard the news about the Declaration of War on the third of September 1939, at eleven o' clock on a Sunday morning. We had stopped work for a short break as the news came from the radio and immediately our work directive changed. With the outbreak of World War Two, Malta became one of the most strategic military bases in the Mediterranean. Many of our senior officers had been sent back to England to train the new recruits, so our troops were thin on the ground at the beginning of the war. Because of this, we worked long hours of heavy manual labour as we reinforced the entire picturesque coastline with barbed wire barricades and prepared to defend against whatever came our way, but otherwise it was a relatively safe position for the first nine months of the war.

We spent months rolling out double layers of wire and then placing an additional layer on top. Gigantic steel barricades or booms were erected across the harbour entrances and gun posts were built all along the coast. We helped the Maltese regiment and local civilians prepare air raid shelters in the rocky terrain, but we did not receive aircraft or additional supplies of food or equipment, so we didn't think of ourselves as being in any immediate danger. But Hitler would eventually need to get to the Middle East for oil to fuel his advancing armies, thus it was vital for the Allied forces to hold the Eastern Mediterranean, including Malta, Egypt and the Middle East. At that time, Spain and Italy had not joined forces with the Allies or the Germans, but their Fascist governments were more aligned to Nazi German thinking and thus we considered them a potential threat.

I took a work detail on a gunship to patrol the Mediterranean for a few months in the winter of 1939 and early 1940. Our job was to search suspicious ships that may have been carrying supplies for the Germans. We usually boarded the ships and then escorted them back to Malta for searching. One night, I was on board an Italian oil tanker off the coast of the Dardanelles in Turkey. I was assigned to stay on the bridge with the captain, but in the middle of the night I took a break, by walking out onto the deck for fresh air. It was pitch black as I made my way to lean against the railings and as I reached forward, for a rail that doesn't exist on an oil tanker, I started to fall overboard. Time slowed down as I saw the dark water coming towards me. Nobody knew I was there and if I went over I knew I would never be found. Somehow, I regained my balance and to this day I cannot believe my luck at escaping from a watery grave. That experience is the only thing I suffered nightmares about for the rest of my life, as I can't explain to myself how I managed to regain my balance. It had been as if, someone had pulled me back from the brink. Of course as a young man I never told anyone about my brush with death and I certainly didn't volunteer for a gunship patrol again after that incident.

Back on dry land in Malta, the regiment had moved out of Mtarfa barracks into gun posts along the coast with the use of only a small barracks and tents at St Andrew's on the coast at Pembroke, just north of Valletta. We used bicycles to travel to and from our posts; nowhere seemed far away on the tiny island and we mainly worked in the northern region only. During April and May 1940, we heard on the radio that Germany had invaded Denmark, Norway, France, Belgium, Luxembourg and the Netherlands, just as Winston Churchill became the new Prime Minister of Britain. Nobody could believe a great nation like France could be threatened and we certainly became uneasy. Malta remained alert, yet peaceful and it was not until Mussolini plunged Italy into the war, as an enemy nation against us, on the tenth of June 1940, that our world changed forever. Malta knew for sure that it was destined to be a prime target of attack, but we were not ready for the Italian threat so close by and so suddenly. Our officers and troop reinforcements were still training in England and shipments of airplanes, guns and food had not yet arrived.

The rest of Europe was already suffering months of conflict, but we got our first taste of the reality of war on the 11th June, just around teatime, when Malta suffered its first air attack by Italian bombers at the dockyards, killing Maltese soldiers posted at Fort Elmo in Valletta. The shock of that first attack never ever really got time to register with me, as wave after wave of bombers came in over our heads. As I stood holding a gun out through a narrow slit in the wall of a concrete bunker the earth shook, the buildings collapsed, the sky lit up and the people screamed. Any boyhood innocence within me came to a sharp, sudden and explosive maturity. There is no telling at what exact point this happened, but over those first days of war my perception of humanity changed forever. There was no choice but to learn quickly how to survive.

My regiment was occupied day and night, manning gun posts along the coast or unloading any merchant ships that managed to make it to shore. It was too dangerous for the civilians to do this work at the docks. The noise was deafening most of the time, but then it would seem so silent in between raids as we waited anxiously for the sirens to sound again. We had three Gladiators biplanes from the First World War christened Faith, Hope and Charity, but they had little effect against two hundred

Italian aircraft based sixty miles north in Sicily. At best, our planes could force the enemy aircraft to bomb from a greater height, but that helped us little down below. By the 22nd of June, France was in Nazi hands and so were the French North African colonies of Algeria, Morocco, and Tunisia. All of a sudden, Malta was completely surrounded by the enemy and besieged, with no supplies able to reach shore because of constant bombing raids from the sky and U-boats in the surrounding waters. So that was my introduction to war, with the bombardment continuing daily for the first six months, with food rations slowly dwindling and harsh, heavy work every day with little rest. I saw my mates killed and injured one by one around me, by explosives and gunfire from the sky. As I tried to come to terms with my baptism of fire and, with human suffering, I could hear myself screaming inside my head at times and I had to teach myself to control my emotions if I wanted to survive.

In those first months there was so much to learn about the strategy of survival and warfare. Each aircraft had a different sound, so the type of attack or what target was most likely could be anticipated. The ground seemed to shake constantly and at night we had fireworks all the time. I remember gazing at St. Paul's Bay where I used to swim every morning, but now, although the sea still glistened in the glorious sunlight as before, the beaches were inaccessible due to the barbed wire and landmines, wreckage and hostile fire from the air. The little coloured boats and the friendly fishermen had disappeared and it was as if the world had turned grey, even though the sun still shone through the smoke in the sky. The villages were silent too, as the locals retreated underground, only appearing to look for food or carry out essential duties in between the bombing raids.

The Maltese civilians minimized loss of life during the war by constructing air-raid shelters and relocating large numbers of the population from the cities of Valletta and Grand Harbour to safer parts of the island. The old railway tunnel between Valletta and Floriana provided a sanctuary for many during the bombing raids. They also used a network of ancient caves and tombs for protection, demonstrating their historic ability to endure persecution and any siege. It would have been easier to hold up a white flag, but they never wavered, despite the misery. These people had endured sieges before and knew that faith and hope eventually leads to salvation. I have total admiration for the fortitude of the Maltese people as they could easily have surrendered the island with a Pro-Italian and church sympathy ticket, but they held fast and taught us soldiers some lessons from the Maltese Siege Survival Procedure Manual. Their ancestors had instilled endurance in their blood, via their genetic makeup or folklore heritage, and it seemed as if suffering was considered a test rather than a persecution against this nation. Malta may not have been in a position to take any sort of offensive action in 1940, but the Maltese people, alongside the Allied forces, proved over the subsequent years to be experts at holding a defensive position, until reinforcements could finally arrive. There was no other choice but to wait, as there was no escape.

Sleeping was difficult at first with all the noise, but I grew accustomed to taking a nap when I felt relatively safe. I must say that was not very often. We lived in a team of six men in a gun post and took turns sleeping and guarding the lookout. We heard the news around July 1940 that Hitler had started air attacks on Britain and intended to invade the British Isles. It made military sense that Ireland would be a useful base for Nazi control of the Atlantic and in fact, after the war, a Nazi document was found detailing the plan to invade Ireland under "Operation Green". Although Hitler stated that he preferred to wait for the Irish Government to invite him in, he must have changed his mind, as it was obvious he had not waited for an invitation anywhere else he had wanted to go. We didn't know how our families back home were managing, but we were concerned about them and now we understood our role in this war and were fully committed to our duty.

It took until August before the Royal Airforce found a safe opportunity to fly in twelve Hurricane planes from an aircraft carrier; I think it was from the HMS Argus. We grew to love the sound of the Hurricane engines overhead as they made some attempt to defend us, but many were obliterated in the sky and we watched them disintegrate into the sea. Faith, Hope and Charity, along with the few remaining Hurricanes, did manage to take out some of the enemy planes and we were very proud of them. We received a few shipments from Alexandria, in Egypt, during September and October 1940 and the one job we men dreaded was the unloading of any ship that managed to enter the harbour. As we swiftly toiled to offload the cargoes, the enemy bombers concentrated all their firepower on the harbour, sinking many ships at anchor with massive loss of life. A watery death had become quite a fear for me, but orders had to be followed and the cargoes represented our only chance of survival. By now, the Italians were bombing Egypt, Palestine and attacking Greece, but more significantly, they were also forming an Alliance with Germany and Japan to become the Axis Alliance.

Hitler made it clear that he wanted Malta as a German base for the North African campaign. If it did not surrender, he gave orders for the Luftwaffe (German air force) to bomb the island off the face of the earth and sink it into the sea. So in December 1940, the, Luftwaffe or more specifically the X. Fliegerkorps (10th Air Corps) moved into Sicily to support the Italians. Now, with over two hundred and fifty aircraft assigned to attack Malta, their combined force greatly outnumbered our few planes. The X. Fliegerkorps played a very different game to the Italians, with their fast flying Junkers JU87 (Stukas) dropping low and cheeky over our heads. At least we could attempt to shoot back, unlike the cowardly Italians in their Savoia-Marchetti's who remained high in the sky and out of our range.

Meanwhile, German and Italian submarines maintained a relentless assault on the supply convoys to the island, but miraculously the aircraft carrier HMS Illustrious and the cruiser Southampton limped into harbour in January 1941. They had extensive damage caused by multiple bombs, but they did deliver their cargoes. We witnessed very few ships after that visit, except for the ones burning on the horizon as they succumbed to aerial or submarine attack and we helplessly watched as all our hopes of food went up in smoke. Over the next few months, we watched as an odd delivery of Hurricanes flew in from the HMS Ark Royal and HMS Furious, but many of those became targets on the ground as well as in the sky and they brought no food.

Soldiers had nowhere to shelter, except in the isolated gun posts along the coast or in trenches around the airfield and harbour. As the sirens wailed, we could easily see the dark swarm of encroaching doom heading our way from Sicily. As the drone drew closer the aircraft model could be deciphered and preparations made for the type of attack. Those sirens continuously wailed day after day, month after month, night and day. The Italians usually opted for high level bombing of the harbours, airfields or military sites, but because of their altitude, they often missed the target. They also attempted coastal seacraft landings, so we needed to be alert in the gun huts. The German Stukas caused us the most bother, as they could fly low and fast, riddling the area with bullets and dropping bombs more accurately. They were not as fussy about legitimate targets as the I-ties (Italians.) When the Stukas first arrived we were terrified as they dropped out of the sky vertically with a penetrating whine or screech. The noise was so scary, especially at night, and I never could be sure they were not coming for me. At night explosions and fires appeared on the skyline, and the rumbling sounded like a thunderstorm, which never blew over. We also had to maintain the airfields by keeping the runways clear after the enemy bomber and fighter planes had retreated. These respites never lasted too long and we had to work fast to repair the craters before we heard the dreaded drone of enemy planes returning for yet another attack. Our guns were generally powerless against the flying destruction, but every so often we managed to hit one.

Gun posts were considered targets, and many times our team had a near miss. The uncertainty eventually became the norm and we just kept sleeping for four hours, looking out for four and surviving the rest of the day. Contact with the outside world was by a wind-up telephone to talk to the command centre to get instructions or report any activity. The wire to the telephone had been rolled out across the ground and I hoped that the goats did not eat it, as they ate everything and were most likely as hungry as everyone else on the island. A supply truck brought us water and ammunition supplies when the skies were peaceful, but it rarely brought food. We each had a bunk with straw and our blanket for a bed. Our kit bag was always with us and consisted of a 303 single shot rifle from the First World War with a bayonet attachment and a pouch with ammunition magazines. It also had a mess tin, knife, fork and spoon, which we very rarely needed. We carried a blanket, rubber ground sheet, and a waterproof overcoat. We always carried a gas mask, water bottle, and wore a tin hat, weapon belt and webbing, which we washed with a paste made by soaking the local sandstone rock in water to make soap.

In any group, a mix of personalities works best. The pessimist balances the optimist from getting too carried away, and the optimist prevents the group getting too depressed. I would say I was the optimist and I always tried to lighten the tense situations, especially at times like a 5am 'stand to' alert when a soldier is at his lowest ebb. I believe strongly that the darkest hour is just before dawn and it is a good time for a wee joke. Many young lads went crazy and ended up in Mtarfa hospital. Sometimes we were sent to the hospital on a work detail to guard these lads or protect them and I do believe it was the most difficult work of all. They had shut down from human contact, to live in another world where no one could touch them or harm them and certainly no one could find a way in to help them. Some lived in a world of tranquilly and others never left the battlefield. I made a vow to myself then, to concentrate on remaining sane by keeping everyone's spirits up, so I talked about home and life after the war and told jokes often at the officer's expense.

Our social life was now revolving around a gas stove in a coastal hut. We used it for boiling water, but we sat and talked about the food we could cook on that stove, if only we had the ingredients. We were so hungry all the time, but these days were a preparation for worse years ahead, as at least we could get some fresh fruit from the neighbouring farmers from time to time. We lads lived on what was called "iron rations". That is, the last resort emergency rations and always from a tin can. We had corned beef for breakfast and maybe again for supper, if we were lucky. When I say corned beef, I mean we had one tin to share among six men. Some days we survived on barely anything at all, even though we were working extremely hard night and day and in highly stressful and dangerous circumstances. The Maltese civilian population, like us, had to survive on very little food during this time. They received their ration of food from centralised feeding stations, which they called Victory Kitchens. That was positive thinking, especially considering the tiny mouthfuls of food each person received from those pots, and making the journey to and from the station was often a nightmare in between raids. We were under siege for nine months with absolutely nothing going out or coming into the port or airfield and the food portions dwindled.

The German flagship, the Bismarck sank the British flagship Hood in May 1941, with the Royal Navy sinking the Bismarck a few days later. By mid 1941, the Germans had invaded Romania and Yugoslavia and had the French territories of Syria and Lebanon in their control. By June, they decided to march into Russia and this offered us some respite as the Luftwaffe disappeared from Malta for a few months to concentrate on the massive Russian invasion. Even though the I-Ties continued their persistent raids on Malta, it felt like a respite and a few ships made it to harbour with cargoes of Hurricanes and wooden Mosquito fighter planes, extra troops, fuel and ammunition, but little food. We did not get any time off duty in the early days of war, but when reinforcements finally started arriving, we got a few hours to go to Valletta once and a while. The towns lay in ruins and if we went to the city, it usually came under attack at least once during the evening, so we always carried our tin hat and gas mask everywhere we went. The cinema was hit one night with some of our lads inside, but the tin hat did not save them. The bars in Malta served a special shot called the Bismarck, which was a very popular spirit, but I stuck to the beer. It was safer to drink beer than water during the war. In July, the Italians got braver and attempted an attack from the sea by ramming the boom defenses at the harbour with torpedo boats and submarines. Needless to say, they did not succeed and all of them perished. In September, more Hurricanes flew in from the aircraft carrier, HMS Ark Royal, and again in November she sent us planes, but on her return to Gibraltar, the hard working HMS Ark Royal was torpedoed by a U-boat and sank.

Beragh and my family were now a long distant, yet vivid memory. I had been away from home over four years and I was a much-changed man from the young lad who arrived in Malta. But somehow I still felt a connection with home; as I closed my eyes to dream of the driving westerly rain on my face and the cool grass beneath my feet, I could hear Mammy calling me for supper. I could see the cabbage and potatoes on my plate, but as soon as I went to taste the most perfect dinner in the world, it simply disappeared. One unusually quiet night I was on guard at St. Paul's Bay and nothing much was happening in the waters below or in the sky above me. My mind was alert, but my thoughts kept drifting back home to my uncle Mick. In fact, I had been dreaming about him a lot lately, as I could see him working away in the shed with the cows or standing at the fire in the old mill. Later that night, I was at my post when I heard the distinctive thud of a man falling to the ground. I don't think I could have mistaken the sound even though I was no doubt hungry and tired. Many men had fallen around me in recent years and I was sure of the sound I heard on that occasion. But there had been no reported attacks that night and a quick sweep of my immediate vicinity found no casualty. It really annoyed me at first, as I came to the realisation in my heart, that I knew my uncle Mick had died back home. I had to wait a further four years to confirm this premonition.

The world was in a real mess by December 1941 as the Germans pushed into Russia, the Japanese declared war on the USA with an attack on Pearl Harbour in Hawaii and Germany declared war on the USA a few days later, going on to sink American ships just off the American coastline. We got our limited news mainly from the BBC World Service and we hoped American troops would become involved in Europe now. Malta's worst period of the war was in early 1942, when the air raids never ceased. The Germans returned before Christmas, with their new toys called Messerschmitt 109's, which dashed our reinforcement hopes, as they, along with the Stukas, crippled our navy. During these months the rain of bombs and bullets could only be described as an Armageddon. The HMS Maori sank in Grand Harbour and on the 15th of February, our Captain Low was killed along with other Irish Fusiliers in my platoon, and that was the day the Regent Theatre disappeared with many lives lost inside. At least they were no longer hungry and were at peace underground.

We started getting Spitfires in early March and the locals and troops alike cheered loudly as the first batch of about fifteen flew in over our heads, from the HMS Eagle and HMS Argus into Ta'Qali under the cover of the Hurricanes. The film named "The Malta Story" details events from this period on, just as the Allies started to build up an adequate offensive force on the island. Otherwise, we were at breaking point and the turning of the tide was a long way off yet. The Gerry's (Germans) main target was the airfields and the destruction of our aircraft and they were very sore on Ta'Qali for a few months. I was one of three thousand men to build huge reinforced pens for the newly acquired airforce and we also maintained the runway on a daily basis. Our home became a camouflaged dugout, with a tarpaulin over our heads. Lice and disease caused major problems in 1942 for the Maltese population and the military, with polio, dysentery, TB and typhoid outbreaks, due to malnutrition and confinement underground in overcrowded spaces with little water or basic sanitary facilities. It was one thing complaining about what we suffered as young strong men, but I dread to think how difficult it was for the families in the underground tombs.

We continued to get small numbers of Spitfires over the next few months and now, with our own planes in the sky, the RAF boys started fighting back a little but we took heavy losses in the sky and on the ground as bombs penetrated the hangers. We simply rebuilt them again and again, as the hailstorm of flying metal and body parts raged around us. From March to April alone, 6700 tons of bombs rained down on the island. The Gerry's and the I-Ties bombed twenty-four hours per day. We could almost see them taking off from Sicily on a clear day, the silver wings glistening like angels on the horizon, before transforming into a black mist above our heads. They averaged three hundred sorties per day and the earth vibrated continuously under my feet, as most of the bombs dropped in my vicinity and never further than five miles away on the tiny island. On Easter Sunday, the city of Valletta was reduced to rubble and many of our soldiers sustained injuries due to a raid on the St. Andrews barracks. Most of the buildings throughout the island suffered damage or were destroyed during the war, 11,000 of them in April 1942, the worst month of bombing. Meanwhile Field Marshall Lord John Gort V.C replaced our commander and chief, General Sir William Dobbie, as an act of defiance to show Britain's determination that Malta would not submit, for if it fell, the Mediterranean Sea would be lost and the North African campaign gravely jeopardized.

That year a special message from the British king, George VI, informed the people of Malta that they had collectively been awarded the George Cross, for their unyielding bravery. It was to, "bear witness to a heroism and devotion that will long be famous in history." Malta earned this unique honour for the heroic resistance of its civilian population in the face of the harshest siege and bombardment of the Second World War. The Maltese suffering was extreme with two and a half years of constant fear, hunger and death. The collective George Cross award remained their unique honour, until April 1999, when the Royal Ulster Constabulary, the police force for Northern Ireland, became the second recipient, as a parting gift from Queen Elizabeth, just before the organisation became defunct.

Malta became known as the most bombed place on earth. Most of this bombing was concentrated in small areas such as the harbour and the RAF airfields where I just happened to spend a lot of my working hours. More bombs were dropped on the island in a twenty-four hour period than anywhere else in history. Nearly fifteen hundred Maltese civilians were killed in the air raids and thousands were hurt. It is a miracle the whole nation was not lost. I was filling in holes at Ta'Qali Airfield during an air raid on 9th April 1942, when the attack became so intense that I had to rise from my position in an existing crater and run into Mosta village for cover. There was not much time to get there before the next wave of Gerry bombers dumped their load, with four bombs hitting the village. I was huddled beside the church as I thought it was a safe place to shelter. As the shells fell on Mosta, one bomb went straight through the dome of the church beside me. There was a crowd of three hundred people taking cover in the church at the time and the bomb simply landed among them and rolled up the aisle unexploded, with no one hurt. The people flooded out the church doors into the mayhem outside, dispersing to safer hiding places. I remembered admiring that beautiful dome and now I thought of it destroyed before I ever got to see inside the church. But when I saw the terrified people running, I leapt up and ran back to the safety of a crater at the airfield before the church could explode around me. But the bomb never did explode.

Mosta Dome is one of the largest unsupported domes in the world and is dedicated to the Assumption of Our Lady. The Feast of the Assumption is held on August 15, a day we had always recognised at home by going to Mass. The villagers of Mosta believe our Lady protected them that day, as they have a great devotion to her. I totally agree with them that I witnessed a miracle in Mosta.

Eventually, in May, we got another delivery of fifty or more Spitfire aircraft coming in from the American ship, USS Wasp. We also received some ammunition, but no food. I got the new job of driving a truck with supplies out to the coastal outposts. Of course it was highly dangerous, but miraculously I never took a hit. Maybe that is why I am not the greatest motorway driver now, as I learned to drive in a perpetual swerving style to avoid craters or falling bombs. I thought it was a much better job than manning a gun post, as shooting at aircraft from the ground was generally futile and the German Luftwaffe, were usually much more successful at hitting us on the ground.

I also refuelled and loaded ammunition and bombs onto our own aircraft at Ta'Qali as we started to get aircraft into the sky and the bullies got a taste of their own medicine. If I happened to be on coastal duty, I would watch for a mine-laying ship called the "Flying Welshman," as it chanced the journey from England or Gibraltar to bring in a few supplies to the island. It carried more military supplies than food so we never got a significant amount of food to feed a nation, let alone an army as well, but it was fast, and to see a ship reach harbour was a ray of hope and better than nothing. The submarine Olympus struck a mine and sank while leaving Malta in May, drowning eighty-nine people, but nine survivors swam the seven miles back to Malta and I often wonder if I could I have swam that far under such horrific circumstances.

By the summer of 1942, Malta was in dire need of food and fuel to continue its struggle against the Axis powers. As the Maltese prayed to Santa Marija, who's feast day was due on August 15th, Britain sent a convoy of 14 merchant ships with supplies, under the armed escort of forty or so warships as part of "Operation Pedestal." As the ships neared Malta, they came under massive air and sea attack. Some were sunk and others had to return to Gibraltar damaged. Only five merchant ships remained, including the oil tanker SS Ohio, with 11,000 ton of fuel on board. This fuel was critical for Malta's survival and the Ohio was badly hit and sinking out at sea. On August 13th, three vessels limped into Grand Harbour, with one more struggling in on the 14th, so more prayers were offered to Santa Marija and on the morning of the 15th, the Ohio reached Malta and the locals gave thanks and declared it another a miracle. She was barely afloat and as the fuel was quickly pumped out of her hold, she slowly sank. The Ohio had fulfilled her mission and the crowds celebrated all along the walls of Grand Harbour. It seems August 15th has always been a significant date in my life and that was a wonderful day, but many men died bringing survival to us. We did not receive another shipment for three months and, for much of that year, the country's civilian and military population were reduced to near starvation levels. Despite this, we managed to hold on and defend the island until vital supplies came through. This relief finally came in the form of Operation Stoneage on the 17th November 1942 with a convoy of four ships, escorted by three cruisers and 10 destroyers. Its arrival eased the misery of the long and bloody siege of Malta.

It is impossible to understand how I lived though that onslaught when many of my mates did not. Unless you have experienced the impact of at least one bomb and seen the carnage it leaves in its wake, I find it is difficult to explain how it shatters your mind, body and spirit. But I guess, when bombs are an everyday experience, a person can develop immunity. Fear of death and destruction became secondary in importance to us, as hunger and deprivation of all that is essential to everyday life became vital. With each close proximity explosion I survived, I simply thanked God I was still alive, shook myself down and threw myself into the mayhem of helping others and as always, clearing up the mess. This constant bombardment was my reality along with the constant pain of extreme hunger and lack of sleep. I was numb most of the time and mainly just thought about when I would see food again. All I thought about was food. I did pray for food, if I got a peaceful moment, but we just seemed to work continuously. Although I did feel abandoned, I knew I was looked after somehow and that knowledge kept me sane during the difficult moments of despair.

By November 1942, the allied forces, under General Montgomery, had some success in Egypt with the New Zealander's pushing the Axis troops, under the formidable German Field Marshall Rommel, back towards Libya. The US Army had similar successes in Morocco, Algeria and Tunisia. If Spain had joined the Fascist Axis forces as feared and had allowed the German troops to pass down through Spanish territory, the story would have been very different, but Franco remained neutral and the Straits of Gibraltar remained open. From November 1942, conditions began to steadily improve as supplies began to get through to Malta. We still suffered countless attacks, but with a little more corned beef in our bellies, we could survive. Countless ships and submarines ended up on the ocean floor just attempting to get supplies to us, many of them lay at the bottom of Grand Harbour. A U-boat sank our speedy cruiser the 'Welshman' off the coast of Tobruk in Libya, as she left Malta on her way to Alexandria in February 1943. On one of her last trips, she brought seed potato to the island and it made me so homesick to remember the great family event of planting the crops back home at the beginning of the busy spring season. The magnificent SS California met her fateful end three hundred miles west of Spain, when three German bomber aircraft attacked her convoy on the way to Sierra Leone on the 11th July 1943. She was abandoned and left burning.

When the Axis forces of Germany and Italy surrendered in North Africa in May 1943, the siege of Malta was finally lifted. A few months later Italy, worn out by the war, officially surrendered to the Allies on the 8th of September 1943 and turned against its former ally, Nazi Germany, who in turn, immediately invaded Italy. So the war ended for Malta, nearly as suddenly as it had started. With North Africa back under Allied control, our position was safer. We may have started the war with little aircraft or offensive capability, but with determination and prayer we went on to play a very significant role in the war as the 'unsinkable aircraft carrier of the Mediterranan'. By May 1943, the Allied forces operating from Malta had managed to sink two hundred and thirty Axis ships in sixty-four days, possibly the highest rate of the war. We also reduced a few of their aircraft numbers and I certainly didn't miss their visits. Despite some air raids by the Germans continuing after May, the British and American troops started arriving to relieve us in June 1943. During one of the final raids, I received a head wound. June had been a quieter month, so one night a few of us soldiers had headed into Birkirkara to socialise. On the walk home the air raid sirens sounded and as usual the locals immediately ran for the air raid shelter beside us. Soldiers couldn't use the shelters and I cannot remember what happened, but I was knocked out. My mates told me I had remained unconscious for two days and I woke in our tent in a makeshift camp at Birkirkara. It was the weekend and they thought I would sleep it off, even though I had a large open wound in my head. There had been rumours that our battalion was moving out in a few days and they knew I would refuse to go to hospital. It seems crazy now, but at that time, after everything we lads had been through together, there was only one thing we feared and that was being separated from our regiment. I pulled my hat down over the wound and avoided the medics.

Looking back now at that decision, I can see that it was another fork in my life path and the decision I made was to prove a grave mistake, I think. If I had resigned myself to a well-deserved hospital bed that day, I most likely would have found myself homeward bound instead of heading in through the gates of hell itself, a hell no man or beast should ever have to endure. But that was the path I chose. I have often wondered how different a person I would be today if I had taken the ticket home as an injured man that day in Malta.

MY TOUR OF EUROPE 1938-45

Chapter Nine

THE BATTLE OF LEROS

Head injury or not, my mates helped McCrystal, as I was called, to his feet and I was standing with them ready for the move forward onto the troop ship Neutralia heading for North Africa. As we left Grand Harbour we met hundreds of British and American ships gathering at Malta before the invasion of Italy. We looked back for the last time at the devastation inflicted on the towering fortifications that surrounded the once impressive cities of Valletta, Birgu, Cospicua and Senglea as they stood in rubble, with a reported thirty thousand buildings having been destroyed on the little island. The sight was nearly unrecognizable from the magnificent harbour that had greeted us five years earlier. Back then these walls had looked impenetrable, having survived a long history of attack by invading armies. Even though they were in ruins now, they had effectively done their job again. They would be rebuilt, as the people were little changed; shell-shocked certainly, but just as resilient as their forefathers and determined to get back up and running as soon as possible.

I had spent the formative years of my youth in Malta and I had left a few mates buried in its rocky landscape. It was sad to think I would never see the island again and more difficult to believe I had survived there. I had survived in the most bombed place on earth in recorded history. We left late in the evening for Tripoli in Libya, where we converged with many other Allied ships. Once the large flotilla was gathered up into a convoy we headed east towards Egypt, hugging the relative safety of the North African coast, sailing directly into the path of a trigger happy German U-Boat. My troopship was sailing alongside another ship carrying troops who were going home on leave, mainly for convalescence. The U-Boat must have been delighted to come across a large enemy flotilla and had no hesitation in launching an attack. A torpedo passed in front of our ship, luckily missing us by about nine inches the captain said, but slammed directly into the other ship, sinking it in minutes with all those men lost just like that. It happened so quickly and thank God we didn't hear any screams or anything, as we knew our ship, containing fighting troops, was the more obvious target. I suppose I could easily have been on that other ship, as an injured man, if I had taken the option to go to hospital. Our ship couldn't stop, as the U-boat was still in the area hoping for another strike, but we got through to Alexandria without any further incident.

I was given a few days to rest in Alexandria before starting work again loading ships at the Port of Sidi Bishr. The mood was upbeat in the camp following the great success in Africa by the Allied forces. The locals were busy rebuilding their lives and the troops had started preparations for the push into Europe. I met soldiers from Australia, New Zealand, Canada, South Africa and India during these weeks and life was fine here as we had food again, although my stomach took some time to adjust. The summer heat really suited me and helped to dry up the head wound. Midday temperatures could rise over 40 degrees centigrade and I was fascinated by all the new culture I saw around me. I noticed the local Arab men rode about on donkeys and camels and the women carried huge loads on their backs. The men also sat around smoking the hookah pipe together in the cafés or on street corners and the women walked about completely covered in black from head to foot. It seemed like a great idea to have a sphinx tattooed on my bare forearm, as a reminder of Egypt 1943. Ann Shelton came to sing for the troops and I enjoyed the relaxed atmosphere in Alexandria, but that respite only lasted a few weeks and before long, we commenced a long arduous trip in the back of a truck across the desert. We thought we might be heading for Italy, but now we were travelling east, passing through areas of burnt-out wreckage, including huge German tiger tanks and we spent a few days on guard duty at a large prisoner of war camp for Italian and German captives. The war was on the turn and maybe I could get home soon.

During this time I spent a night sleeping under the stars, in the shadow of the great Pyramids at Giza. If I hadn't been in the middle of a warzone, I possibly might have appreciated the significance of this moment more, but I specifically remember gazing at the stars, as I lay on the sand with the Sphinx silhouetted nearby. Detailed memories of this time are vague, as I suspect I had not really recovered from the knock on the head and I was still physically weak from years of starvation. My head wound healed, but I was suffering from headaches as we spent a month in the desert loading aircraft with ammunition and fuelling them with Octane for bombing raids elsewhere in the German-held territories of southern Europe. We then commenced training for an operation to push into Europe, although we did not yet know where. Before long, we were travelling by truck from Cairo, over the Suez Canal to the Sinai desert, through Gaza, Haifa, Beirut and finally stopping in Tripoli in Syria. We came all that way for "Mountain Warfare Training" and I can tell you, it was hard work. On completion, the Brigadier told us: "The Faughs are as much at home on the mountains as they were on Malta". That is about as good an army compliment as one can get. After training at high altitudes in Syria, we moved to Jenin in Palestine, which is below sea level near the Dead Sea, for low altitude exercises and combined operations training using pretend landing craft. We also learned about rock climbing on a quarry face. By early August, we went back to Egypt to practice our landing craft skills for real on the Suez Canal near Kebrit. I specifically remember swimming in the Suez Canal while stationed there as it was my last time ever to swim for pleasure. I was a strong swimmer and luckily I had learned during the good times in Malta as the opportunity never presented itself again.

Finally, we moved back to Syria and then Palestine, and I found myself in the familiarity of Haifa city by the 16th of September 1943. Palestine was more habitable and familiar than the desert of Egypt and it felt like an old friend. I had spent time here in 1938-39 and the people and culture were reassuring in some strange way. Haifa provided us lads with the opportunity of a few nights out and after a beer or two we could imagine nothing had changed since 1938. But the beer could not erase the fact that we were all changed and many of the old team were missing from the bar stools around us and now we faced an uncertain future again. As individual men, the training had us as fit and strong as horses again, ready to form a feeder group, to support any front in Europe that needed troops. We were fit but secretly scared, wondering what our next mission might entail. Churchill wanted to secure the Greek Islands before the Germans following the surrender of the Italians based there. Churchill also thought a landing in Greek territory might distract attention from Italy as the Germans might think we were establishing a base on the Greek islands. The Allies were doing well in Italy by this stage, and the Americans did not want to jeopardise the Italian campaign and so decided not to offer assistance to British forces in Greece. Therefore, we were chosen for the suicide mission of spearheading the landings into the Greek Isles alone. Well our battle cry was 'Faugh À Ballagh' or 'Clear the Way' after all.

By now we formed part of the 234th Brigade, made up of about 3,000 men, but belonging to the 2nd Battalion of Royal Irish Fusiliers was all that was important to me. We were 'The Faughs' from Malta, serving under Lieutenant Colonel Maurice French, whom we highly respected and we were happy to follow his lead. We were also joined by the 4th Battalion of the Buffs (Royal East Kent Regiment) the 1st Battalion of the King's Own Royal Regiment (Lancaster's) and the 2nd company of the 2nd Battalion of the West Kent Regiment. In late September 1943 we received anti-malaria treatment and with little detailed information, we boarded a troopship in Haifa heading for Rhodes. We diverted at the last minute as Rhodes was swarming with Germans who had won the race to the island with the airfield. So we moved on north to disembark from landing craft onto the beaches of a small island called Leros instead. Some of the men, including Colonel French, took ill from sand fly fever on the first days after arriving. Thank God it missed me. Situated a few miles off the Turkish coast, Leros is one of the twelve Dodecanese Greek islands situated in the Aegean Sea. Italy had occupied this island until now as the natural inlets provided excellent anchorage for Italian submarines, flying boats and warships. Thus, our Allied forces had been constantly bombarding it since 1941 or so. As we arrived, the Italians had surrendered and had half-heartedly joined the fight against Germany so we had nothing to fear from the surviving Italians in the gun posts on Leros, but could expect little help from them.

Leros was even smaller than Malta, measuring only 14km long and at most 5kms wide with a narrow central neck only 1.5kms wide giving the island the shape of an egg timer. There must have been another strategic interest in this island other than distracting attention from the Italian landings when so many of us had been consigned to this mission. Now that the Germans had beaten us to the airfield at Rhodes, we had little hope of ever receiving back up as our planes had to fly the long distance from Africa or Cyprus with our much-needed supplies and ammunition. We wondered why we had ended up in this quiet backwater and why on earth any army would want this island. The only thing this mountainous, rocky place was good for was goats—lots and lots of goats!

Well, it turned out we knew nothing. Rhodes or Kos would be useful to an army as an airforce base, but Leros had a deep harbour suitable for ships to launch an invasion into the Balkans or Greece and push the Germans back. The Nazis wanted to move into the Middle East for the oil they so desperately needed for their war machine and Turkey was the only country in their way. The Turks, having remained neutral this far, now found the war was at their borders, but nobody was keen to take on the Turks. So these islands were necessary to enable the Nazis to skirt around Turkey. Leros was only twenty miles away from the Turkish shore and the Nazis had had no concerns about this area whilst in Italian control, but with their surrender in September, the

Germans would be determined to claim the Aegean islands for themselves and Britain knew it. This mission was to be a trap and we were the bait, but once we knew the Germans had the airfield on Rhodes we should have known the mission was doomed.

Maybe Churchill hoped the Turks would help us out, but that hope failed and I found myself on this very rugged and mountainous island with little tree or even foliage cover to protect me. Before we dispersed from the beach, our Welsh Catholic Priest, Father Anwyl, held a quick service and gave us all the last rites, so we had no doubt about what to expect. After Malta we were no longer naïve about war. Each regiment spread out over the tiny island and my 'A' company climbed up on the high ridge, to the south of the central narrow-necked section of land between the bays and dug in for the long haul. Well, we didn't exactly dig in because we were sitting on bare rock and having no huts or tents; we had to use our blankets for shelter. The local Greek islanders had long since disappeared underground and I saw few Italians around.

The plan had been that, once we were in our positions, ammunition and supplies would be dropped to us at night by aircraft. We were not properly armed to defend this island as we only had an ancient 303 rifle from the First World War and one Bren machine-gun between six men. Any ammunition had been carried with us up the mountain and that would not last long. We may have had a few Bofor and AA guns high in the mountains and along the coast, but we certainly had little protection from possible air attacks. Like in Malta, we were to find out the hard way just how passionately the Germans wanted this island of goats. It did not take long for them to find us and, after a couple of quiet days, all hell suddenly broke loose as we heard the old familiar drone of Stuka 87s and 88s heading our way. We were sitting ducks, on an open hillside, so the best we could do was spread out, lie as flat as pancakes under our camouflage and pray during each sortie. We knew from experience in Malta that these aircraft could drop down low over our heads so fast, therefore earning their name 'Stuka', which is short for "SturzKampfFlugzeug", meaning "Diving Combat Aircraft."

In between attacks, the six of us took turns sleeping or on look out, but usually we stayed in position and called out to each other, instead of gathering together. The first disaster was the loss of the destroyer, HMS Intrepid and the Greek navy flagship, Olga, at anchor in the bay directly below me. They were blown to pieces by JU88 bombers as I watched in despair and thought, "Here we go again". The bloated bodies of men from the ships washed up on the shores of Leros for weeks. Another destroyer went down within days. The RAF was unable to provide air cover as planned because the Germans had captured the airfield at Cos, as well as Rhodes, giving them complete air superiority. We waited every night for supplies, but we never got a delivery as the Gerrys had no intention of letting our planes in, even under cover of darkness. Therefore I spotted very few friendly aircraft, but what I do know is that the German Luftwaffe's JU 87s and JU 88s were happily bombing us and riddling the area with bullets. All that saved us was our camouflage, complete stillness and the luck of the draw. Of course, that did not save everyone.

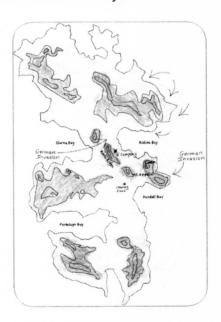

MAP OF LEROS 1943

I was in 'A' company of the Faughs, holding a position on a barren area of rock on the mountains to the south of the neck of the island, an area that we called Charing Cross, overlooking the Gurna and Alinda bays. From my perch up on the ridge, I could see the four central bays when I was sitting up or standing, but that was not too often. Our job was to hold off any coastal landing craft in the bays below us. I had a view of the sea all around me and what a view it could have been if only the skies and water had been free of twisted wreckage, exploding bombs and dying men. I think we were up on that hillside for well over a month and although we were easy targets, sitting out in the open rocky landscape, my section managed to stay alive and sane. As the weeks passed, I became extremely hungry and I slept very little, as bombs kept waking me up. The runners brought us our water rations at night, but little food. Facing the pain of hunger again is more difficult when you know from experience how bleak the future looks. We knew no support was coming, but we settled in to keep the Germans busy. We had been well trained for this mission and we had the advantage of being the most experienced battalion in a siege situation, therefore despite the lack of food and supplies, we survived the impossible from late September until the 12th of November. The Royal Navy had stopped the German invading fleet once, by sinking many ships below me. The Germans attempted to invade the island a second time, and this time they succeeded. The defense of Leros was disastrous for the Royal Navy as four submarines and six destroyers were sunk and the cruiser HMS Carlisle was very badly damaged.

In the early hours of November 12th, 1943, a combined sea and airborne force of elite German troops invaded the island by separating into two groups to approach the island from east and west. The Germans quickly succeeded in cutting the island in two across the flat narrow neck section. I could not believe my eyes at the vision of German Paratroopers risking life and limb to land on this mountainous terrain. The planes came in low over the sea in straight rows, well below our Bofor and anti-Aircraft gun positions high on the mountains. Then the Junkers suddenly rose up as they approached the flat neck of the island. The sky was black with parachutes as the elite German Brandenburg Division jumped in their hundreds from the JU 52s. I really had to admire their determination, for we thought a parachute landing would be impossible but here I could see maybe over five hundred men dropping in around us. We commenced firing but they were on the ground in no time at all. I was completely penned in from below and our communication between the north and south of the island was cut off. We continued fighting for five days, but we had no air support and were completely outnumbered and abandoned. Our section decided to spread out across the hillside and lay very flat and still to the ground, to avoid the low flying aerial guns spotting us. Eventually the Bren gun ran out of ammunition and we were defending our position with a single round ancient rifle, but somehow we held the elite soldiers off for five days.

The last official report we received from command was that we had permission to attempt to reach the beaches and escape by boat if possible, but the sights I had seen in the waters below convinced me to stay on my belly and on land. I had no desire to be lost at sea and my intuition told me to forget the boat idea. More and more, I was learning to trust my intuition, even when it flew in the face of reason or the easy option. We could no longer call out to each other in case the Germans heard us, but I could hear the familiar sound of 303 rifles around the hillside. I was now completely alone and, as the bombs and bullets rained down around me, I had no idea if my mates had survived each day. I have no heroic tales of combat to tell except that I stayed at my post and held back the enemy advance. What I couldn't know, without communication, is that the Germans were also advancing uphill from the bay behind me. The tin hat of water I used to wash my face in was congealed with soap, my water bottle was near empty and I was so hungry. It was just an impossible battle and I knew the loss of life around me must be heartbreaking if I could lift my head to see it. The lads in my company were like brothers and we had been through many a scrap together over the years, but we couldn't even bury our friends in this inhospitable landscape or drop our guard long enough to crawl around to find them. But the enemy also suffered heavy losses in those last few days on Leros.

It was then that I came face to face with the German enemy for the first time. On the last day of battle, as I lay on that ridge, everything seemed eerily quiet. We had kept the enemy well pinned down below us and I could see no movement coming up the hillside. I couldn't hear any friendly fire from my company either or maybe I had fallen asleep. All of a sudden, as I lay on the ground with my ancient gun tightly gripped in my hands, I found myself surrounded by enemy soldiers pointing machineguns at me. Yes, they had modern machine guns and we had antiquated rifles. It is a big difference to hold a position at a distance than to actually look the enemy directly in the eye. Up until that moment, I had been defending against a faceless enemy who attacked in the form of metal bullets and bombs from aircraft, ships and submarines. This had been mostly a one-way attack on me, with little opportunity to counter-attack. Then, as I watched these German paratroopers hover above me, I could see real men, just like me, sent to fight for a lump of rock in the middle of nowhere. I had no choice but lay down my rifle. They helped me to my feet and patting my back they said, "good fight, good fight". They had no interest in revenge, even though we had been shooting at them all week. I realised then that these lads were sons and brothers to others and that we all wanted to return home when this war was over.

During that six-week mission in Leros, I had been trapped in a nightmare of horror as I was forced to make moral choices with my moderately accurate aim. The hell is not in the gruesome sights you see around you on the battlefield, it is in the conflict inside yourself as your body demands survival and your soul demands justice and your heart struggles between anger and compassion. Many men have broken down in battle and, of course, many others used battle for revenge. A soldier is very much at the mercy of these types within their own ranks and within that of the enemy. Commanding Officers, fueled by revenge or madness have led many good men into suicidal or genocidal missions. I often thank God for not putting me in such a cruel position and I hope I passed the moral tests of combat. At least only soldiers had been involved in this battle on Leros, in proper combat between trained men, well away from innocent families. In doing my duty, I prayed I had not taken anyone's life, as I had decided at the beginning of the war that I would try not to kill anyone deliberately, yet I understood that any bullet or shell had the potential to kill. I believed an injured man slowed an army more effectively than a dead soldier and I deliberately aimed not to kill. Some people may wish to disagree and say that killing is the duty of a soldier, but remember that your conscience will demand justification for every action in the long years ahead. In Malta I had searched for people in the rubble and I clearly understood that finding a man injured, rather than dead on the battlefield, made all the difference in the world. Even though soldiers have little choice in battle, it is still possible to have moral integrity as well as doing the job as instructed. I couldn't understand how these Germans could have dropped bombs on the children of Malta, but I had more to learn about the capability of humans in a war situation.

Because of our failure in Leros, thousands of Greek Jews and civilians from those islands were rounded up and gassed in concentration camps and that is difficult for me to accept. War certainly brings out the best and the worst in people and no one really knows how they might react when war threatens their life and then offers them the bait of survival. That is how good people end up doing bad things. I believe that all war crimes should be investigated and justice and truth revealed, but I would not want to take the moral decision to deliberately take a life in retribution. It is difficult to find solutions for evil without hardening your own soul. Lieutenant-General Mueller aka 'the Butcher of Crete' had commanded the German attack on Leros and ended up executed by the Greeks for War crimes in 1947.

We surrendered on the 16th of November after six weeks under attack and five days of siege. I realised our Colonel was dead along with most of my company and all of my section, as I never saw any of their faces again. I left my dead comrades on those hills for the Germans to bury, set down my old rifle and relinquished my freedom. That was a joke—as if I could refer to the past five years of my life as free. In a way, it was a relief to lay down the guns and not have to defend a position anymore. I had been without any sleep, food or ease for such a long time. As I rose to my feet, I stumbled and swayed. I had not been upright for weeks and my head spun. I was relived to sit down again with other prisoners, at the beach and wait to see my friends arrive. They never came, but I found some of my regiment. The German soldiers were nice enough as we had put up a good fight and they respected that. These were German paratroopers, an elite force of fighting men. They appreciated the battle we gave them and they made us aware of that. War ethnics are a strange affair. They gave me a 2oz tin of my old favourite corned beef to eat, as that awful stuff appeared everywhere during the war. We lads often debated about what corned beef was actually made of and I won't say what we decided, but once the war ended, I never tasted the stuff again.

The advantage of being a prisoner of war is that decisions are now completely out of your control and I could finally close my eyes and sleep. No more action for me. What a luxury sleep can be, even on the steel floor of an old ship. The soldiers all discussed the fact that at least the Red Cross will send food to a POW. The siege and starvation of Malta had left us all obsessed about food and the cuisine of Leros had rendered us quite skinny by now. I have often wondered if my war-weary regiment from Malta was the right force for the Greek offensive. It would have been fitting to leave us in Malta instead of replacing us with fresh men there and sending us on to a new frontline. After three years of siege, constant battle and starvation we could not have been the best battalion for any strategic assault, but then again we were experienced and hardy. We knew the Greek isle spearhead invasion was to act as a decoy for the landings in Italy, but we didn't know we were to be sacrificed likes lambs (or should I say goats) for it. Estimates say 700 Allied troops and many more

German soldiers died in Leros and Kos during those six weeks, but war estimates are always conflicting between sides. All I know is that I lost most of my friends and the loss of our highly respected Lieutenant-Colonel Maurice French was an additional blow as he was brave and fought side by side with his men. But we had done the job we were sent to do well enough and, although that battle was lost, it played its part as the war was won some eighteen months later. It was reported that the German's captured approximately 3,500 or more Allied troops during that Dodecanese campaign and I was now part of that statistic. The Ministry of Defense assumed I was missing in action, presumed dead, and informed my mother. I was now off the radar in the land of the living and I knew no one was looking for me. I was twenty-three years old and all I thought about was the fact that at least I received the last rites and I hoped to get food some day soon. Other fellas desperately needed a smoke and it is a wonder I didn't start smoking then, but I would have eaten a cigarette.

Chapter Ten

PRISONER OF WAR

As we gave up our weapons and came down the hill, we surrendered to an enemy who had yet to show us the true extent of its dehumanization policies. We were taken to mainland Greece, battened down in the hold of a German merchant ship. During the voyage we were concerned about the possibility of an attack from our own side, but we arrived safely. We stayed in Athens for a few weeks, held in a big open compound guarded by guns. I have no particular memories of this time as I operated more like a robot in the camp, but I was pleased to see Walter Pancott and some other fellas from our regiment in the crowd. My headaches tortured me, so I think I slept a lot. We were marched through the city as part of a propaganda campaign by the Germans. During this parade some of the prisoners talked about chancing a break, by running into the crowd of Greek onlookers. As we marched through the streets for hours, a group of squaddies beside me started debating when to make a run for it and they asked if I was on for it. So here I was again, facing one of those life or death choices. I hardly had the energy to think as I was suffering a terrible headache as we marched due to the head injury I received back in Malta three months before, - to think of all the countries I had seen since and all the battle, death and destruction I had faced since then, it was no wonder my head hurt. As I looked at the faces of the Greek onlookers, I wondered if they would protect me or turn me in. Where could I go for safety and most importantly, would there be food? A voice in my ear kept telling me to stay in the parade. So when my colleagues made the break and disappeared into the Greek population, I just kept on marching. I will never know if that was the right decision because, to this day, I don't know if any of those boys ever made it home.

The officers and men were separated in Athens, but our boss, Colonel French had died in combat on Leros and his brother was also lost in action. Of course, he was later decorated after the war for his bravery, he just wasn't there to know it or receive his medals. I suppose the medals went to his family in Wexford. Lieutenant Hugh Gore-Booth, of Lissadell House in Sligo, also died on Leros as an officer of the Royal Irish Fusiliers, as did his brother in another regiment. The famous poet, W.B Yeats was a friend of their family and wrote a poem about their famous aunt, the Countess Constance Gore-Booth Markievicz who was sentenced to death for her part in the Irish Republican Easter Uprising of 1916 against the British in Dublin. The sentence was commuted because of her gender and she became the first woman to be elected to the British Parliament in 1918 but, as a Sinn Féin candidate, she refused to take her seat. Her father, Hugh's grandfather, had been an English landlord during the famine, proving that the divisions in Irish political opinion are deep-rooted, within the very fabric of all our families, so no wonder we are a very confused nation of people. Our passion for justice often found us driven to opposing views on how to achieve it. Passion, rather than strategic planning, drives the Irish, which may be romantic and beguiling, but is disastrous in a war situation. I wondered how I had found myself in this position when I didn't even know what I believed in myself when I was only seventeen back home. I wished I'd had known more back then, but one thing I did know by 1943 was the fact that this war would have eventually pushed its nose up against mine, whether I met it here in Europe now, or if I had waited at home until Hitler's army arrived on my family doorstep to raid the homes of Tyrone. In 1943, most of the world was in a very dark place and everywhere people lived in fear.

I was sent with the other squaddies on a long train journey right up through Europe. It wasn't exactly the Orient Express and I certainly did not find myself in the First Class cabin. Instead, fifty men at a time were loaded into actual cattle trucks behind a train. We were so tightly packed, that if one man turned everyone had to turn. There was a bucket in the corner for a toilet. We spent fifteen days in that trailer, with little food or water. Some days the train stopped and let a trailer or two of men out for walk around, but the guards usually worked this operation starting from either the front or the back of the train and unfortunately, my trailer was in the middle section, so we often missed out. This was a miserable journey to hell, or maybe worse. How could humans be treated like this? In later years, I discovered that civilians, including women, children, babies, the sick and elderly, had suffered this same journey to Nazi hell camps all over Europe.

Our train travelled up through Greece, Yugoslavia, Hungary, Austria, and into the heartland of Nazi Germany. We were still in our tropical uniforms, with short sleeves and trousers made of light material, so as we moved north we became very cold. I remember reaching through the bars for long icicles off the roof of the cattle truck, just to get a small drop of fresh water. We were all so very hungry. No, hunger is too mild a word for the starvation we suffered, as I don't think we had seen a proper meal in years and now we had nothing but a few bits of bread and water. I was on a train bound for God knows where, I knew few of the lads around me, I was so weak and I thought I would die of that headache. Still, I kept calm and thought about all the lovely meals I had eaten at home. I tried so hard to remember every detail of my life in Ireland. How could I have complained about runny custard all those years ago? I remembered every bite of food I may have wasted. Survival during those fifteen days and nights on that train can only be attributed to my Guardian Angel, the little voice I heard in my ear when I needed guidance. Otherwise I think I would have curled up and died. Well, I would not have been able to curl up, but there was very little to live for at that time and I could only hope that things could not get much worse.

Eventually we arrived at Stalag 7A at Moosberg, just north of Munich in southern Germany. This was an old disused garage, which had been made into a holding camp for processing, interrogating and distributing prisoners of war. There were prisoners from all over Europe and this was my first introduction to Russians, Poles, French and Italians. Well, I had met some Italians down the barrel of a gun in Malta a time or two, but now we were all here together, all different nationalities and all enemies to the Nazi regime that held us captive. I remember vividly the first night we spent there. An Italian prisoner had broken into our compound looking for food he thought we might have brought with us. When I woke in the morning he had hung himself on the door of our hut. All hopes of a better life here flickered and died and I succumbed to the pain in my head. Processing was a methodical German assembly line operation, with the taking of our details, shaving, delousing, fumigating our bodies and giving us an allocation of a winter uniform from the Red Cross. I am sure they were dead soldiers' clothes, but I was glad of their warmth. These were British Army uniforms, with a red diamond sown on the knee and back shoulder. We were given flat metal tags for around our necks, with our new POW numbers engraved on them. Luckily I was not selected for interrogation, as I really don't think I would have survived that torture, as I was now quite ill.

Within a few weeks, we were loaded back into the cattle wagons and the train headed northeast deep into German territory. With no information and less hope, we filed into those wagons, on a train bound for nowhere-the only relief being that the journey only took a few days. Our train, full of humans, was of secondary importance to German troop or artillery cargoes. Our wagons were shunted to the side to let any other important cargo through on the busy lines, thus we ended up in the sidings for many hours just waiting for the tracks to clear. It is not great for morale to realise you are the lowest form of life. Well, it was only after the war that I understood that many ordinary people from all over Europe and Russia had been treated much worse than us. Finally, late one night, the train stopped and the doors opened. The sign above the large gateway announced that our new home was to be Stalag 4B, in a small village called Mulhberg, in the East German heartland. Stalag 4B was a huge camp for tens of thousands of men. Some say as many as eighty thousand men were detained there. I suppose it was near the Polish border and many of the prisoners were Polish and Russian.

Most of the Polish men had been prisoners from the start of the war and they were practically corpses by late1943. Even the local dogs were smart enough to stay out of the camp. The Germans had hundreds of prisoner camps all over Europe and they were all categorised with a district number and a letter for the specific camp, such as 4B. There were also different camp names, according to the type of prisoner held there, for example I was in a Stalag, which was for enlisted men, and NCOs (non-commissioned officers.) A Dulag was a transit camp, a Oflag was for officer class, the airforce were sent to a Stalag Luft and there were many other prisoner camps, such as the KZ or concentration camps for ordinary men, women, children and babies, who the Nazis simply decided to murder, imprison or work to death.

Many of the western European countries and America had signed up for membership of the Geneva Accord in 1929, prior to WWII, thus protecting their troops to some extent while detained as prisoners of war. One of the requirements was that POW camps must be open to inspection by authorised representatives of a neutral power, such as the Swiss Red Cross, and also allow the Red Cross to support the prisoners with food parcels. The accord demanded that POW camps have adequate heating and lighting in the buildings. Enlisted ranks like me could be expected to work, as long as it was not dangerous and did not support the captor's war effort. The work should be generally agricultural or industrial, mining, quarrying, in mills, in factories, railway yards, or forests. POWs hired out to military and civilian contractors were supposed to receive pay. The workers were also supposed to get at least one day per week of rest. Sergeants and above were required to work only in a supervisory role. Commissioned officers were not required to work, although they could volunteer. The captors were also to ensure that POW's who died in captivity were honorably buried in marked graves. We discussed our plight and decided that, with this Geneva protection agreement, we might be safe and hopefully get food more often than we did as soldiers.

In the dreadful and overcrowded conditions of Stalag 4B, the starving men of different nationalities were kept in separate compounds for ease of management and to avoid internal feuding. Unfortunately for the Russian and Polish prisoners, their countries had not signed up in 1929 and they did not receive a weekly Red Cross parcel, so they suffered a cruel existence compared to us. As a compensation for the lack of Red Cross support, the Germans kindly allocated extra food to these unfortunate prisoners, supposedly doubling the rations normally received. So they should have dined in style by sharing a loaf of the German bread between two or three men instead of our five-man portion and, instead of receiving an eight ounce cup of soup, they should have received fifteen or sixteen ounces of soup.

During those years I became a descriptive culinary expert as I imagined wonderful tasting foods from home, but to this day, I cannot describe the vile taste of that German soup, so getting a larger helping was no great pleasure—we thought it was made from boiling old boots and rotten cabbage. Even with the soup, we were all so hungry that we often searched through the dustbins hoping to find anything edible—frantically I would pray, "give us this day our daily bread"—but I never found anything.

It was nearing Christmas and things just kept getting worse. Shortly after we arrived, the German officers lined us new boys up and asked any Irishmen to step forward. The Irish Free

State had remained neutral during the war and therefore was not an enemy state to Germany. Among the crowd there were many fellas from the Irish Free State, serving in the British Army and most of them stepped forward. Northern Ireland citizens are entitled to an Irish passport and citizenship, as well as a British passport and citizenship, so it was logical to think that this selection might be some chance of a release ticket, so the lads from the North also stepped forward. Again a voice told me to stand my ground, even though I could see Walter and other fusiliers in the forward group. Maybe I was just too ill to make the move or face a decision, but I stood my ground, with only one other Irishman. The others were marched away and out through the gates, leaving Jimmy Butler from Wexford and myself remaining as the only Irishmen in that camp.

The rest were moved to an Irish sub-camp and survivors of the Irish camp later told me that they were treated very badly by the Germans who firstly asked them to join the Nazi army as Irishmen against the British and when they refused, the Nazi officers reckoned they shouldn't have been fighting for the foreign British army in the first place and called them traitors. In hindsight, I may have made another good decision, but I also thought I might never survive in this overcrowded camp. Malnutrition and disease did not care about nationality or faith, or about who you might have been before the war. The men around me were dropping like flies and, for weeks, we were carrying the dead out every few minutes. Eventually a miracle happened, as within a few weeks, Butler and I were offered the opportunity to volunteer for a transfer to a labour camp, which turned out to be a much superior hotel. Well, I might as well be doing something instead of going off my head with boredom, cold and hunger in Stalag 4B.

Winter is bleak in Germany and I had chosen the wrong time of year for sightseeing. Through the narrow slits of the cattle wagon the flat countryside rolled by until we eventually stopped in a small village called Hartmannsdorf, situated somewhere between the cities of Dresden, Leipzig and on the outskirts of

Chemnitz. Stalag 4F was much smaller and less crowded than 4B, with the main camp serving many smaller sub-camps or kommandos. We spent many nights in various kommandos when we had work detail in the cities or at a local factory or reservoir. Well, I don't remember much at first, as I collapsed and ended up in hospital for three weeks. It was a miracle I had kept going all the way from Malta—I had been determined to stay with the familiarity of my battalion, but, after finally arriving in this permanent camp, I did not need to fight anymore. I had seen many of my close mates killed or simply disappear into the mist of war. I had no one really close to look after now, so I could quit. I had reached my final destination and there was nothing left to strive for. I was completely alone in this alien world, with foreign languages all around me.

After my collapse, the German guards placed my stretcher into a railway wagon and one guard stayed with me, as the train pulled away. They told me I was going to a POW hospital or in their words, "Lazarett fur Kriegsgefangene." So even in the midst of all this fear and deprivation there was kindness, along with a Guardian Angel, who would not allow me to quit.

Along the way, we stopped for a while at a factory. I could see the white smoke coming out of the chimney and the smell was indescribably sickening. The guard was very jumpy and indicated to me in sign language a cutthroat movement. I was too ill to care. Of course, after the war I knew what the guard meant about the factory. It was a human extermination factory and the smoke was from human flesh and bones. I am glad I was naïve of that fact at the time.

As far as I know, the hospital was in a village called Hohenstein. The ward had about six American soldiers already hospitalised when I arrived. As ill as I was, I tried not to let down my guard while I was awake. Even though I was only semi-conscious, I do remember one traumatic episode. The surgeon came to take fluid from my spine; I think he said 47 drops. I really don't know what happened, as one nurse lay across my head and the other across my legs to hold me down. He must have run out of anesthetic, as it was the most painful procedure I have ever experienced or ever hope to experience. I can't remember any conversations with the Americans or any details about those weeks. Slowly, I recovered enough to get about the ward and looking through the window, I could see corpse after corpse leaving an area further down the corridor. It was time to get better and even though the headache had not improved much, I was conscious and moving. It was a relief to get on a train and content myself that it had delivered me back to Stalag 4F.

I returned to the hut with Butler and the other semi-familiar prisoners and survived, somehow, for a further eighteen months. I cured the headaches with Aspirin and boiling hot cloth bandages. Maybe my mother was praying for me. I could not remember the faces of those loved ones back home and they could never imagine in their worst nightmares what this place was like. It was a tough life and boys simply aged overnight. I remember one young fella coming in with a head of black hair and by morning he had turned grey. I don't know if that is possible, but that is how it looked to me.

The winter was so cold, and the snow so deep, that we had to dig our way out of the huts some mornings. There was one central stove in the centre of the bunkhouse for one hundred and fifty men and the winter of 1944/45 was extremely cold. During the night, the condensation would freeze on the ceiling and fall like rain on us in the morning as the sun hit the roof. The sub zero temperatures of mainland Europe in winter can be very cruel on the toes, especially when their only protection was a cloth wrap for a sock and a clog made with a wooden plinth tied to the foot with a leather strap. For a man who had enjoyed nothing but sunshine and heat for six years, I now managed to survive two extremely harsh winters working outside every day digging reservoirs, building huts or clearing rubble with no protective clothing of any sort. Not even boots on my feet. Then the summer could get so hot, but I loved the heat on my back as I worked.

Food was a constant concern. Breakfast consisted solely of black coffee. Later in the day we received our daily ration of 250 grams of bread. This was black bread and if you squeezed the water out there was nothing left at all. Some days we got soup for dinner. The soup was coloured water and it filled you with nothing but wind. We simply would not have survived without our weekly parcel from the Red Cross. Oh, how we waited for that parcel. Contained in that package I would find a Bar of Chocolate, concentrated milk powder, 10oz tinned meat or fish, egg flakes, 2oz of sugar and tea, Horlicks and biscuits. The Canadian parcels were the best and the ones from Slough in England were the worst. Often it contained a bar of soap, sweets and of course, it always had fifty cigarettes. As I didn't smoke, I could barter mine for other useful things or sometimes I just gave them to my distraught friends. It was no surprise; I suppose, that the first parcel we received was just too rich for our poor bodies. The milk and chocolate just ran straight through us and out onto the floor. I remember the cramps in my belly, but it did not stop me trying the food again the following week. I knew my body needed this nourishment and it definitely was the only chance we had of survival.

Once a year, the Red Cross sent a different parcel with underwear and socks if you were lucky. Socks were a real luxury item made back home by kind women who put nice things into a Christmas Red Cross parcel and sent it to us. I suppose a little like the shoebox appeals for the third world of today. On Christmas Eve 1944, we were told a priest was coming to say Midnight Mass for us and we were delighted but of course he never showed up, so Christmas ended up just like any other day of the year expect we talked about turkey and stuffing and what might be happening at home. Someone played the accordion and we sang, but the spirits could be described as very low that evening. Contents of the parcel depended on what country you hailed from. The British and American parcels were the best as they contained luxury items, which practically represented hard currency in war torn Germany. The Russians, Poles and Italians got nothing and many of them simply didn't survive.

The German guards and local town folk suffered greatly too due to war rationing and happily traded our luxury items for bread. The price was controlled by the supply and demand for items. Lucky for me, I always had a few cigarettes when an opportunity presented a loaf of bread.

The Americans received Old Gold or Chesterfield cigarettes and the British had mainly Flag cigarettes. Each brand had a different value in a fluctuating market but at the end of the day, the German civilians and guards relished any brand. Sometimes a packet of twenty cigarettes would trade for perhaps two loaves but mostly only one. Our soap, sugar and chocolate could also be traded. "Verboten" was a word we heard often from the German officers. Translated to English verboten means "forbidden". It was forbidden to trade with the German civilians, but the hungry German guards could be bribed. The black market was necessary for the impoverished German population. Credit had to be given to the German guards as they always ensured we got our Red Cross parcels when they easily could have benefited from them.

The Nazis ran a very disciplined and organized Army that played by most of its own rules. It is the rules you have to question. I still find it difficult to fathom their clear-cut confidence in a superior race and how simply they relegated every other human race and creed to a sub-human status. Everyone was catalogued and categorized by the Nazi scale of importance and we were very lucky that American and British Commonwealth POWs seemed to be high up that category list unlike the Russians and Polish.

There were men from countries all over the world in our camp such as Australia, New Zealand, Canada, South Africa and most European countries and we got on well with each other. We had devised a democratic form of government, which worked extremely well. If we got a loaf of bread or anything else too small to share we simply drew lots with a double set of playing cards. Firstly we would cut the loaf into the thinnest possible slices and then everyone took a card from one deck. The matching cards drawn from the other deck won the prize.

Our spokesman was a South African guy, as he was best able to communicate with the German guards. I also attempted to learn as much German as possible from the guards in case it would come in useful later and it also kept my mind active. Our guards were old or injured soldiers and mostly give us little trouble if we give them little trouble, but we dreaded to see the Hitler Jugend (Hitler Youth) coming about the camp as they were very nasty. I made sure I didn't attract any attention when these children held the guns. Even the parents of these young men were afraid of them as they often reported family members for any criticism of the government. Hitler believed that the future of Germany was its children. He stated: *"The weak must be chiselled away. I want young men and women who can suffer pain. A young German must be as swift as a greyhound, as tough as leather, and as hard as Krupp's steel"*. The Hitler Youth catered for 10 to 18 year olds and was a compulsory organisation for boys and girls. The boys prepared for military service and the girls prepared for motherhood and had to be able to run 60 metres in 14 seconds, throw a ball 12 metres, complete a 2 hour march, swim 100 metres and know how to make a bed. I suppose it is understandable why they were so nasty as they had no childhood.

In the camp I kept my head down and caused no bother. All the lads still tried to keep fit by clearing snow and walking about, but we had little muscle remaining on our lean bodies. Every Saturday we were marched away for a good shower. It was really hot like a sauna and it was such a relief to shed the itchy clothes. At least it was one thing to look forward to in the week. Our clothes were deloused and fumigated, but the whole operation was pointless as we climbed back into the same dirty bunks along with the bugs that night. Years later I watched film footage of the extermination of so many people in the concentration camps and I was horrified that all those innocent people thought they were going to the showers, only to be gassed to death. All I can picture in my mind are those Saturday mornings when I too trusted my guards as I was marching to the shower. The most overwhelming emotion about survival is guilt. The hardest part is knowing that you survived, while millions of innocent people didn't.

The long months passed with most of our days spent out digging a reservoir for water to put out the fires, and we had all become so thin due to the heavy manual labour. The social life was great though! We sat about together trying to keep our spirits up by singing songs and telling stories. The stories revolved around our lives back home and the great meals our mothers used to make. There was nothing else to do and in some ways it was better than armed combat and bombs dropping on your head everyday. It is much like saying that you have a choice between hanging and the firing squad—I am sure one is better than the other, but neither is very appealing.

Chapter Eleven

THE BOMBING OF DRESDEN

Towards the close of 1944, we could distinguish the sound of increasing Allied aircraft activity over Germany, prematurely raising our morale and inflating our hopes of seeing home again some day soon. We could start to dream about a chance of freedom. But as more of us died or went insane with disease, malnutrition and overwhelming despair, that hope faded at times. Ever since the German blitz bombing campaign commenced against British cities in the early Forties, the Allied forces had striven to give the Germans a taste of their own medicine. This was characteristic warfare logic. By the beginning of 1945 the Nazis were on their knees and Allied bombers had access to bomb German cities by night. I must admit we POWs rejoiced at the sound of our planes flying over our heads as we anticipated the end of the war. At night we could hear the bombing of nearby towns such as Leipzig and Chemnitz and often our work teams were sent out to clear the rubble. This was hard physical work for starving men but it was better than losing your mind with boredom sitting around in the camp.

Dresden was not a military base and was known as a hospital city and surrounded by many prisoner-of-war camps and thus it was assumed an unlikely target. Therefore, when the sirens sounded at 9:55p.m on the Shrove Tuesday night of February

13th 1945, the people of Dresden may not have rushed down into the shelters before the first bombs fell at nine minutes past the hour. That night, I was in a Sub-camp of Stalag 4F somewhere about forty-five miles from Dresden and I heard the drone of the bombers heading east and about thirty minutes later, I heard them flying west again on their way back to England. As we lay in our bunks, we had decided they sounded like hundreds of Lancaster bombers. Dresden was ablaze and the wind whipped those fires into a firestorm that engulfed the city. We were woken by aircraft overhead again before 1 am on their way to bomb the city again and I remember we stayed awake until we heard them return and fade into the distance. Little did we know that the fires in Dresden burned out of control and turned into a fireball inferno. In the morning the Americans flew in the same direction over our heads. With thoughts only of ourselves our spirits soared as we anticipated our libration from this hell.

With the raid over, for the salvage work in Dresden, the Nazis relied on some 25,000 Allied prisoners of war like me who were concentrated in and around the city. The Germans could not cope with the clear up operation so we were drafted in to dig the mass graves and bury the dead. It was winter and the ground was frozen. We were just skin and bone, but we dug and dug. The bodies just kept coming. One load after the other of men, women, children and babies were dumped beside us. They came in buckets and they came in bags and they just kept coming. The bodies were piled up in two long continuous rows and we dug a central trench between them. Then we threw the bodies in and covered up the trench. There were no prayers, no tears and no words. If I was ever near madness, I have to say this was the time. These people were dead from our so-called friendly fire. It was difficult to see a victory in those trenches. I was barely surviving physically myself, yet alone able to try to make any sense out of the situation I was in. I just kept going in total faith that at best I would get fed that day.

We were told that Shrove Tuesday was usually a great festival time in Dresden with a carnival to celebrate the beginning of

Lent. But on February 13, 1945, the Russian Red Army was only sixty miles away from the city and advancing. Knowledge of this transformed the festive mood into an anxious fear of the looming Russian invasion. The city streets were no doubt crowded with refugees who had fled from smaller towns and villages like a wave in front of the Russians. These people had horror stories about the atrocities they had witnessed. I can now appreciate their fear as I myself witnessed the Russian invasion of a German village a few months later. Families were camping in the bitter cold, wondering where they might find sanctuary in the days to come. They certainly couldn't return home to the East and all other directions led straight into the path of our advancing Allied forces.

These German civilians were suddenly exiles in their own country and may have been naïve as to why the world was so angry with them. But as the Allied forces advanced from the east, west and south, further and further into German territory, the soldiers discovered the barbaric treatment of ordinary people and prisoners in hospitals, prisons and concentration camps. The first-hand sight of this calculated policy of mistreatment and extermination of whole races of people by the Nazis must have left the librating armies distraught and their initial anger turned on the German population. The innocent always seem to get caught in the middle with nowhere to run and Dresden was packed full of such people.

Silence was the best company during the first days of this work, but as the weeks progressed into months of digging we did hear some of the details from inside the city. I thought I had seen it all in Malta but listening to the stories and bearing witness to these bodies, I thanked my lucky stars I was not consigned to the salvage teams in the city. The fire had consumed all the oxygen in the air-raid shelters and most of those people would have died quickly either by total incineration or melting into a thick liquid. We were told it was horrific but many of those shelters were never opened or never even found under the rubble above. Tens of thousands had fled to the great open space of the Grosse

Garten, the huge central park of Dresden. They were sitting ducks here as a second raid commenced without warning, after 1 a.m. There must have been twice as many bombers overhead and I heard later that in a sea of flames the only dark area was the rectangular shape of the Grosse Garten and the river, which made an easy target from the sky.

Rescue squads and fire brigades made their way to the stricken city immediately after the first raid, from all around the suburbs, just as the second wave of bombs began to fall. Most of the rescue teams also perished in the firestorm or got crushed in the panic. By 11:30 am the following morning, the third wave of bombers of about two hundred American planes began their attack and the survivors also talked about Mustang fighters diving low and shooting at the bodies on the banks of the River Elbe and the lawns of the Grosse Garten. Other Mustangs targeted the crowds that blocked every road out of Dresden. Some of the bodies had come from a huge water tank near the Market Square. There had been a sudden stampede to escape the heat of the fire by plunging into it. The sloping sides were slippery and the people eventually sank to the bottom. The tank was not discovered until five days later, and all rescuers found were bloated bodies just like the ones I had seen in the sea at Leros. The square was full of bodies practically reduced to ashes.

Many weeks after the raid there were still thousands of unopened cellars under the smoldering ruins, and the air was thick with the stench of rotting flesh. The S.S. made the decision that moving the bodies by horse-drawn carts from the city to us in the surrounding cemeteries was not fast enough to prevent an outbreak of plague, especially as the weather warmed up with the onset of Spring. So it was decided that the rest of the corpses must be disposed of quickly on funeral pyres constructed in the city, the bodies were piled with straw between each layer, soaked with gasoline and set ablaze. Thousands of corpses were disposed of in this way. Afterwards, the ash was loaded into containers and buried in a grave pit outside the city, twenty-five feet wide and fifteen feet deep.

Over those two months I was to witness first-hand the destruction wreaked by that Allied attack and forever remember that German civilians also paid the price charged by war. Well over a hundred thousand civilian people were wiped out that night. Over the subsequent years the propaganda reports from each army have deflated and inflated this number from ten thousand to five hundred thousand lives. All I know is that, no matter what heroic stories are told about war or what wonderful speeches are made to justify a war, the bottom line is always the same. A war always ends with too many beautiful, innocent people thrown in the trenches.

Chapter Twelve

A BLACK HOLE

As I lay in my bed in a cold wooden bunkhouse, I listened to the distant sound of carpet-bombing and thanked God I was safe tonight. Thoughts of living under that constant rain of bombs and bullets in Malta and Leros still tormented me. No matter how dreadful my existence as a POW now seemed, at least sleep was possible. Some nights the bombing came close and no one slept as the sky lit up with flack and fires. But the worst night was on the 5th of March as the bombers came for our neighbouring town of Chemnitz and once again the bombs fell around us.

We could hear the tank battles by this time as the Allies moved slowly, closer to us. Although I should have been optimistic at the sound of encroaching friendly fire, I had lived through too many battles to be naïve about the dangers of the enemy's dying kick. Nearly as worrisome was the threat from the Allied so-called friendly fire as our camp was just on the outskirts of Chemnitz, which was prone to Allied bomber attacks. Often the British and American strategy was to bomb the outskirts of a city first to take out the reservoirs, factories, trains and power lines, so our village of Hartmannsdorf with a large factory base and reservoir was a prime target. Our camp sat right next-door to a huge factory and the train track. During those attacks I think we only lost one prisoner due to shrapnel wounds, but it still felt a little like being back in battle, only this time we had no protection from our own army and we were caged prisoners.

One particular day we had marched out of town to work on the construction of fifteen or so wooden huts to house German refugees, most likely. We had just taken a break and retreated into the shelter of one of those huts for a rest when we heard the American bombers approaching in broad daylight. As soon as we heard the first bomb dropping we all instinctively sank to the ground and lay as flat as humanly possible while many more bombs followed. It was a good sign if I could hear the whistle of the bomb dropping, but, if there is no noise and just the intense sucking sensation of heat, things were not so good as the explosion was sure to be too close for comfort. The lower to the ground or below it you could lie, the better chance of survival. The blast always travelled upwards so it turned out there were some practical advantages to being so very thin. Anyway, on that day we all survived to return to our work. On stepping out of our shed we found nearly all the other fourteen buildings had disappeared during the attack except for the one we had sheltered in so we had to start all over again.

It was some years later before I understood the precarious geographical position of Stalag 4F. Deep in eastern German territory, Hartmannsdorf was one of the last areas to be liberated as our troops invaded Germany from the West and the Russians pushed through Poland from the East to finally meet along a line that ran near my prison between the Elbe and Mulde rivers. By mid-April most of Europe and Poland had been liberated and the world had already witnessed the horrors inside the concentration camps and hospitals. During April, the two mighty armies moved closer and closer until they were nearly face-to-face with the ever-defiant Nazis and us trapped in between. Hitler and his supporting officers may have been losing the war but they had not lost all control of their army. Seeing the writing on the wall, Hitler ordered his troops and the German people to hinder the invading forces by destroying the German infrastructure of power stations, factories, food stores and evidence of war crimes. Hitler was so crazed at this time that he told his Minister of War Production "if the war is lost, the German nation will also perish. So there is no need to consider what the people require for continued existence." He also issued a directive to his forces to wage war without consideration for the German citizens. And I, Paddy, was a POW, the lowest form of life, right there in the middle of hell itself.

The area was descending into mayhem with German people and soldiers running out of fear of the Soviet Red Army. SS men were roaming in gangs, ready to shoot any regular German soldiers who had deserted. I may have been a simple squaddie following orders but I was not stupid nor naïve. It was clear to me I was a sitting duck trapped in a prisoner of war camp. I had survived this far by watching my back carefully and thinking ahead. A few of us discussed our vulnerability and the risks of escaping. As the front line came closer I was so afraid of ending up in one of those mass graves without a name. We knew the Americans had set up camp some weeks previously at the other side of the river, but curiously, they advanced no further. We were desperately waiting for them in a highly anxious state of mind. History tells us now that they were waiting for the Russians because of a political deal made about the land sharing of post war Germany. But, the awareness of the American presence so near was frustrating for frantic prisoners and the temptation to run was too strong to resist. So in desperation I made an uncalculated attempt to escape from Stalag 4F in early April 1945.

A mate of mine, Collins from Manchester, and I had made a vague plan of escape and waited our chance. We could hear the American gunshots in the near distance and knew the direction we wanted to go. One day, we were on a work detail, screwing together wooden huts at a site a few miles from the camp. As we marched back at dark, both of us took up positions at the back of the group and when it was safe we simply threw ourselves into the ditch and waited. Then we took off cross-country until we came to a road to follow. Well I suppose we were missed at the camp and a German search team found us on that road very close to the bridge during the second night. I guess the American guns sounded closer than they really were. It was a foolish reckless move. If the Germans didn't shoot us the Americans probably would have when we tried to approach them. Maybe I was lucky to get caught, but at the time it did not seem so.

As punishment, I found myself in solitary confinement for twenty-one days in a six-foot by four-foot cell. I had been taken blindfolded in a truck some distance from our camp and I do not know exactly where. There was bread and water but no one spoke to me for those twenty-one days. I was now in very bad shape and I was frightened that I would be forgotten in the confusion and never found. Only the enemy guards knew I was interred in that dungeon. What if a bomb fell close by and everyone left? With faith and hope I held on to my physical life and my sanity also. I slept and prayed, waiting out those twenty-one days. I prayed to see my family again and if I ever got home I would never leave the shores of Ireland again. I could hear my mother sing Danny Boy and tell her tales of Tir Na Og and fairies.

The only reasonable explanation for my survival in that black hole can be summed up in the word love. Years later, I read a quote by Mother Teresa of Calcutta which clarified that sense of belonging I felt encouraging me to hold on to life:

> ***Being unwanted, unloved, uncared for,***
> ***forgotten by everybody,***
> ***I think that is a much greater hunger,***
> ***a much greater poverty***
> ***than the person who has nothing to eat."***

I knew my mother, my father, my sister and brothers were willing me home with their thoughts and prayers. So many young lads had come to the army to escape difficulties at home and did not have that love to encourage them on. They were the lads I had given my extra cigarettes to as I could see the emptiness in their eyes. As I watched many of them disappear from this earth, I wondered if anyone cared or grieved or knew what they had suffered. By this point in my life I better understood the lads we had guarded in the hospital at Mtarfa. They had retreated to insanity to survive in a cocoon of safety away from the stark reality of life. I knew their eyes had seen different horrors from mine, either in their childhood or in the rubble of Malta. Their retreat was just another form of survival until they could cope in this world again.

Solitary confinement was a cocoon of sorts for me away from the crazy existence of facing another day of gruesome sights and inhumane atrocities in the camp. Most of the time I was too weak and hungry to think any rational thoughts, but I did know I was loved and my family were waiting for me in Beragh. I drifted in and out of reality, but I could discern if I was still alive most of the time. It was pitch dark in the cell and the only chance I had of counting the days was by mentally noting the times the guard pushed in bread and water in exchange for the chamber pot through the narrow door slot. I always kept alert to the details about time and date in case I would slip from reality. The earth still shook as the air raids continued, but thankfully not too close by. People wonder now what I thought about during those days, completely removed from reality and I have to be honest and say nothing. My mind was numb, as hunger saps all resistance from a normal functioning brain. The Nazis knew this very well as they starved millions and subdued them to become the workforce of the German war machine. If a person gets just enough water and food to survive they will be motivated to work in the hope of more food. Nazi doctors had been experimenting in hospitals for years to discover just the right diet for workers. The hospitals also gave doctors and scientists free rein to subject prisoners to horrific experiments for medical and military advancement. People were frozen alive, injected with diseases and mutilated. Twins were used as medical rag dolls for genetic discovery. Women were used in breeding camps, particularly in Norway, to create the prefect blond, blue-eyed race while Jewish and gypsy women were sterilized for experimentation. Yes, hunger is a great sedative and once you pass a certain point, your mind is very open to suggestion. In later years I have often thought about that, in relation to hunger strikes by prisoners—at what point are they operating with free will and when are others justified in intervening to protect them medically. Anyway, in April 1945 the German guard was giving me just enough bread and water for survival and extending just enough hope of more tomorrow. My only purpose for living was to remain alert for fear that I might fail to hear the guard come to my door. I knew the war was coming to an end some day soon and all I needed to do was survive.

From Failure Up

Under that flat, flat grief of defeat maybe Hope is a seed. Maybe this's what he was born for, this hour Of hopelessness.
Maybe it is here he must search In this hell of unfaith
Where no one has a purpose Where the web of Meaning is broken threads And one man looks at another in fear.
O God can a man find You when he lies with his face downwards
And his nose in the rubble that was his achievement . . . .

Patrick Kavanagh

Chapter Thirteen

LIBERATION DAY

The night before I was released, a British pilot was put into the cell next door. The walls were thin and it was such a relief to speak to someone, especially in English. He had been shot down that day in a field nearby. Our camp had never received new American or British soldiers during my time there. I suppose the Germans didn't like the prisoners to hear the current news from the frontlines. Anyway, Stalag 4F was well embedded in the Eastern heartland of Germany far from the frontlines until recent weeks. He told me not to worry, that the war was nearly over and the Americans were camped at the edge of the Mulde River for the past few weeks and the Russians would reach the area within hours.

The next day I was removed from that cell just as the Germans were considering evacuating the camp. The pilot from the cell was nowhere to be seen. Maybe he had never been real, maybe he was an angel sent to keep me from falling into the abyss of despair at the darkest hour just before the dawn. Now, in the glare of the sunlight I wasn't even sure where I was in the camp. Everything was a blur in my mind as I stumbled along in a daze searching for something familiar to focus my thoughts. All my friends were gone and to this day I've never seen any of them again. Just like all the rest, they disappeared into the ether of war and if they survived, like myself they never dared revisit that episode to search for lost friends in case they couldn't face what they might hear. We were like brothers for a time and I always hoped they found a good life after the war in all the different countries they returned to.

While I was interned in that cell, many things had changed. The combined forces of the Allied Armies had taken Berlin and Germany and the Nazi Regime was on its knees. President Roosevelt had died in America and Mussolini and Hitler were both reported dead. After twenty-one days of solitary confinement, during some of the most significant days in world history, I crawled out of the hole into chaos. It was May 6th 1945 and I had no idea where exactly I was in this strange camp in Germany. But the panic around me quickly brought the realisation that, in a war situation, the last few days can be the most dangerous as no law or order is enforced.

Totally alone, I stood there, dazed by the overpowering sunlight and the absolute chaos about me. Where I found the strength to walk I will never know, but walk I did, in search of a friendly face but nothing seemed familiar in the camp. It did not dawn on me until many years later that I had been released back to a different camp. After wandering about the camp for some time I finally spotted Collins. He had just been released from the hole as well and we debated where our mates could be. We were so hungry and I remember spotting a field of newly planted potatoes beside the camp, so we crawled and reached under the fence and dug up the soggy seed potatoes and some nettles, ate some before we found a pot and lit a fire to boil them up. How had I not see the potatoes before? It bothered me that I didn't recognise anything in the camp or any other faces so I resigned to the fact that I had lost my mind that day. The guards were frantically running around with the dogs yelping by their sides and the prisoners were all very edgy, but Collins and I didn't care, as we searched the huts and found a bunk and slept. I knew the advancing armies were close as the din of the battle raged somewhere in the near distance beyond the barbed wire fences, but still I slept.

The next day, all hell broke loose and everyone was running about in the mud as the guards shouted orders and shot into the air. We both ran, but before we got to the perimeter fence the SS soldiers rounded us prisoners up for a march to a safer German territory away from the advancing frontline. At that time the guards did not know they had nowhere to run as we were surrounded by the Americans to the west and the Russians to the east and these two colossal armies were just about to meet in triumphant victory, squashing the dying kicks of the Nazi regime. Nevertheless we started marching out of the camp and down through an unfamiliar village. We slowly dropped to the back of the crowd. A lad beside us suggested making a break for it. I had everything to gain from this idea as I knew I could not survive marching any distance. So in the middle of the village three of us prisoners slipped into the open doorway of a house and gently closed the door. We turned around to see the man of the house wave us in and we sunk to the floor. Also in the room sat a woman and two little girls. I am sure they were very frightened, but the man opened a bottle of brandy and gave us all a drink. We hunkered there all night, not knowing what was happening outside. The Americans had made no advancement into the village for weeks and it transpired that during that night the Russians liberated the area instead. I crouched in that little kitchen with strangers in a semi daze, assisted and sheltered by a kind German family who I never knew before or after that night. I do believe they were all angels sent to guide me home.

Daylight brought a new level of savage horror as, through a tiny window, we viewed the chaos that reigned on the street outside. The Russians had suffered catastrophic losses ever since the German invasion of their country in 1941, and the Russian Red Army was now hell-bent on revenge against the German people. They intended to dash all German plans of breeding a master race. As their mighty force had surged forward across the German border, they had systematically raped and brutalized all in their path. We could see through the window that mercy was not going to be considered; whether innocent or not, any German was fair game. That is the problem with revenge; as it lashes out at everything in its path, often it is the defenseless and innocent who suffer the retaliation. I am not sure if the three of us agreed to take a chance, to walk out of that house and into the village street, but that is what we did. I still think of that lovely little family we left behind and pray they did not suffer. A British officer came over to me and said, "Get out of here fast. If the Russians get you you'll end up in a salt mine in Siberia and never be seen again. Get away over to the American side lad immediately." So as the Russians attacked the women folk of that little village, we simply started walking until we reached the American Camp. Nobody gave us a second glance; it was as if we were ghosts floating past.

As we entered the safe confines of the American camp I screamed with joy and all thoughts of exhaustion disappeared for a short while. I was on top of the world as we queued for food at a little wooden hut and everyone was giving out cigarettes. I had stumbled upon the 76th Infantry Division of the United States Army who had reached the Mulde River on the 16th of April. There they had gone into a defensive position to hold a bridgehead across the Mulde, near Chemnitz. It must have been their gunfire that attracted me in my foolish dash for freedom. The reality quickly occurred to me that I could not have possibly survived a crossing of that bridge that night in April without drawing bullets from both the Americans and the Germans. Yet again I had been saved by a strange twist of fate. The German enemy had a habit of saving my life, first in Leros, then in hospital and then by throwing me in a hole for twenty-one days.

The Americans immediately moved us freed men into trucks for transportation to a nearby airfield and into the body of an American Dakota bomber. This was my first time to fly or even step inside an airplane. It turned out to be an extra nerve-wracking maiden flight due to a drunken pilot who came out of the air like a dive-bomber over Reims in France. Well I suppose dive-bombing was second nature to him and he may not have considered the greenhorns in the back. Of course, many of those pilots lost their sanity along the way too. Once safely on the ground in France, I took a deep sign of relief. The war in Europe officially came to an end at midnight on the 8th May 1945, just over twenty-four hours after my release from that cell. Thank God someone opened that cell door and let me out.

My one and only night in France was spent in a large country house with a body laid out on a bed in one room. It must have been a wake house. I made sure I stayed in another room for the night. None of us were in party mood because any elation we may have felt about liberation and freedom quickly waned under the influence of exhaustion and hunger, aggravated by foolishly eating too much—the food just ripped my insides apart. The next day I boarded a British Lancaster bomber for the trip home. This was a lovely smooth flight and the crew opened the back cargo door to let us view the beautiful green countryside of southern England below us. I use the word 'us' although I knew absolutely nobody around me except for Collins, yet they felt like family.

My final destination was Barnsley in England. The war in Europe was over and I was safe. What a relief to throw away my filthy POW uniform; have a proper bath and this time climb into a clean soft hospital bed. A soft bed had been missing from my life for years and I think heaven will feel like that moment when my head touched the pillow in Barnsley and I slept so soundly. The feeling was so heady and comforting. I was ordered to take complete rest, along with the other survivors and we were gently reintroduced to food with a strict diet of light milky meals until our bodies could tolerate food again. When my tummy eventually settled down to enjoy a full meal, it felt like Christmas. But it was only the ninth day of June and the World War still continued to rage in the Far East against the Japanese and as an enlisted man the east would be my next assignment. Back in 1937 I had signed up for what the Army called a Seven and Five. That is seven years active service and five years in the Reserves. At Seventeen I had had no idea of time or what lay in store for me, but even though now I did, I could not change my path. As a Reserve you must remain in active service when the country is under threat, so there was more work for me yet, but not until I had a recuperation holiday.

Chapter Fourteen

SURPRISE HOMECOMING

Once I was deemed fit to leave hospital, I was sent home to Tyrone for a six week holiday. It was definitely well overdue and deserved, even though I do say so myself. As I travelled back by cattle boat and train to Omagh, I felt as if I was in a trance. I was still in uniform, as I had no civilian clothes to my name and my new boots felt like sheer luxury. With war rationing I was unlikely to have any civilian clothing for a long time to come. During the war in Malta, my cool Civvy cotton suit had been given away to the locals.

When I arrived home to Beragh, my parents were so upset to see me and, at first, they were very overprotective, as if I were a child. I didn't know that they had received a telegram from the Ministry of Defense the previous year, to say I was missing in action and presumed dead. It must have come in the months after the Battle of Leros. My Mother later told me she didn't believe the telegram, as she had, in desperation and grief, gone to a Gypsy woman, with a crystal ball to ask about me. My mother was able to describe the prisoner of war camp to me, telling me things that happened there accurately, things that she could not possibly have known otherwise. The Gypsy lady had assured her I was alive.

Many things had changed in the eight years since I had innocently waved goodbye to my family as an excited eighteen year old, on a cold December morning in 1937. It shocked me to see my mother looking older and I know she was distraught at the state of my appearance. Those six weeks at home passed very quickly. There wasn't a party as such to celebrate my homecoming, as they were still living on war rations. I don't think I would have had the energy for a proper party, but it was so comforting to sit with the family and neighbours at night around the turf fire, close my eyes and listen to the familiar hum of the chatter and singing. I also relished the Beragh countryside in full summer blossom as I walked the lanes and fields of my childhood memories. Everyone had a ration book full of coupons, which allowed them to buy a limited amount of scarce products such as food, paper, clothes, wood and petrol. I was awarded double food rations at home as I was so thin and malnourished. My mother improvised and begged to find good food for me and made a great fuss. I must say it was comforting to belong to a family again and I really enjoyed that special time with Mammy as she spoiled me rotten. I told her about the Red Cross parcels and how they saved my life and she told me that Mrs. Watson, the doctor's wife in Beragh, had organised the parcels here.

During those weeks I soaked up all the news about the last eight years at home and about my community's experiences of the war. They had stories of rations, blacking out windows at night so German bombers could not see them and about American troops stationed in Omagh. In fact, a large army camp had been built in Omagh during the war and there had also been a POW camp in the town for German soldiers. I hoped they had been treated well in my homeland. It was amazing to hear that German bombers had blitzed Belfast, and that Dublin and other towns in the Free State had also been hit. There were great stories about the Sugar Train from the Free State. The people of the north had been smuggling many goods like sugar, tea, meat, cheese, sweets, butter, margarine, milk, jam and eggs that had been tightly rationed in the North during the war, but were available in the South. The train bound for the seaside town of Bundoran in

Donegal was always packed full of people with their heads full of plans and ingenious tricks for getting their purchases back home across the border. When the guards entered the carriages women hid food under their clothes or used string to hang the goods outside the opposite window to the platform. A border is a great advantage really and my community knew how to utilise it to its full potential. We still benefit from the border to this very day, using the exchange rate between the Euro and Sterling to get the best deal. It was all very exciting and I listened intently to the tales of hardship, but I never told them much about my experiences.

I was a stranger to my younger brothers and it was nice getting to know them again. The youngest, Gerry, was now nearly seven years old and I had never even met him before. He lamented that his knees had been damaged with all the prayers in the chapel Mammy made him say for a person called Packie whom he didn't even know. He asked me if I could stay at home and save his knees. It was great to see Lizzie again and meet her children. Peter was twenty-one years old by now and Francis was seventeen, Desmond fifteen years and Bernard was fourteen years old. It was definitely odd at first to share mum with all these grown up lads, but soon we got to know each other and the family settled down to a new normality. Sadly, I discovered that my premonition about Uncle Mick's death back in 1941 was true. He had died just around the time I had heard him fall in my thoughts back on Malta. I was asked by friends and neighbours 'What have you been doing with yourself all these years Packie?" It seemed as if I did not have the power or energy to tell my story. It did not seem like an interesting tale to me. My mother understood a little of the horror I'd been through from the gypsy lady and she was reluctant to hear much more. I think people were afraid to hear the facts, so in true Northern Irish style, I answered the few questions politely and made a light joke about the war and made the most of this precious time at home. It was a surreal time of overwhelming emotions of belonging. Everybody knew me; they knew my family and my roots. Sure, I was a little older and thinner, but I was the same lad they always had known, except for a few people in the village who didn't recognise me and reported me to the police as a stranger. The police came to question me and we all laughed when I told them why I was in Beragh. I should have spoken in German to them and pretended to be a spy.

The stories about my wonderful life in beautiful places among the amazing people of the Mediterranean prior to the war had faded to grey in my mind and the excitement of sharing those experiences no longer seemed relevant. I was no longer that innocent boy. On the surface, I suppose a person does not change that much, but what others just couldn't see was the weight of the burden of understanding I carried. I understood the unbearable suffering and terror that human hatred can cause. Thank God these people in my home community had not suffered a Nazi invasion. I don't think they realised how close it had come to their door. They definitely did not understand the full consequences of an occupation under 'Operation Green' or how different things could have been if the discussion at the Nazi Wehrmacht Situation Conference of 3 December 1940 had materialised beyond the words of "Der Besitz Irlands könne das Ende des Krieges herbeiführen." In English that means, "The possession of Ireland could hasten the end of the war".

Northern Ireland was a British occupied state and certainly it had Civil Rights issues to be addressed. I could understand my community's lack of respect at having one of their own in the British Army, but deep inside I was proud I had played some part in protecting them against the extreme persecution of this war and they could remain in their ignorance of its nightmare. Everyone was happy I was home safe and life went on, so I kept my enlightened opinions to myself. Many families in my community did not have a son returning home alive to them. One lad from Beragh in my squad had lost a leg and returned to Malta to his Maltese wife. Many fellas married good Catholic Maltese girls and either returned there or settled in Southern Ireland or England, rather than come home to ridicule or abuse. Some had swapped nametags with dead soldiers and left the army as reported dead men and assumed new identities. We lads who did come back home learned quickly not to expect any sympathy or appreciation from our own people. Then one evening, I met my uncle Patrick and aunt Sarah at a pub in Omagh and he commenced one of his stories, but this was a new one on me. I had the feeling they had asked me to meet them there, to confirm their recognition of my adulthood and because it was time for Uncle Patrick to tell me about his Army days during the First World War and how he got injured in the Dardanelles in Turkey. He had got shot through the ear, thus explaining the hole. I was amazed by this revelation by my namesake, as I never thought of Uncle Patrick as being anywhere but here, at the mill, all his life. For all his storytelling, he had kept this one quiet. I expect he told me then because he understood the reaction I was experiencing and it was his way of letting me know that all would be fine eventually and people would forget I was ever a British soldier. We met up in Omagh regularly in the following years for long debates and storytelling.

I was lucky, I suppose, that I had returned home relatively unscathed to a welcoming family. I had no loss of limbs and I was still clinically sane. I had no diseases or addictions and no guilt of consciously taking innocent life. Yes, I was unharmed and I had survived and returned from hell itself. It took me years to rationalise all that stuff out in my head and find peace again. Death had always been close by in my life. As a child, with the loss of four siblings, I suppose I became a prankster, to divert attention from my grief. I had been running free, but with a pain in my heart that I could not voice. But I had always felt protected by a higher spirit and had found my own way to survive in the countryside. Nature is a wonderful healer and in childhood the river, trees and open spaces were my medicine. Now, I needed them all again to calm the confusion in my head. But I could not wander the healing landscape of Beragh forever.

During those weeks at home the Americans dropped the Atomic bombs on Hiroshima and Nagasaki, but the war still raged on in the Far East. My time of convalescence was coming to an end and I was feeling strong again. On the morning of the 15th of August 1945, I said my goodbyes and prayed I would be home again soon. A strong faith in those prayers gave me the strength to get on a bicycle, with a small bag of my meagre belongings, and head for the train in Omagh. The hugs were tighter with this parting. I would take the train to Belfast, a boat to England and then a trip to the unknown, to face the Japanese. As I cycled down the Hospital Road towards Omagh, a few nurses came running down from the Tyrone County Hospital in great spirits. They were hugging everyone and I stopped as they shouted to me, "the war is over, the war is over" They gave me a great big hug and I stood there stunned.

In shock, I left back the hired bicycle to McSorley's hire shop in Bridge Street and walked up the hill to the Courthouse to see an old friend who was a caretaker there. Bobby had left the Army injured years before and I could depend on him to have the current news updates. He had heard the radio reports and it turned out the nurses were right; the war was finally over and a public holiday was granted for forty-eight hours. So I was on holiday again. I didn't expect my prayer to work that quickly, but my mother got to see me again sooner than she ever thought possible. The big relief was that the war was over and I could relax.

With the war over, the Protestant men in Beragh were treated as returning Heroes, with homecoming events in the Orange Hall. One of my army colleagues invited me to come to one of these events with him. The Orange Order gave him five pounds, but there was nothing for Wee Paddy. I really could have done with that money at that time, but I was from the wrong side of the community. No one was interested in my story, so I just decided to keep my mouth shut and melt into the culture I belonged to before the war. Stories of bravery and medals were as useful to me in my community as the ones Colonel French had received after he had died on us in Leros.

In the North of Ireland at that time you either belonged to one community or the other. Unionists and Nationalist lived alongside each other in peace most of the time, but socially there were little opportunities to share common interests. Everyone understood if you fitted into one box or the other, but if you confused that norm with a mixed marriage or affiliating with the other side culturally, you were looking for trouble. I thought differently now I had been out in the world mixing with so many nationalities and just couldn't see the differences in people. But I was being forced to conform to a side if I really wanted to fit back in. I was tired of trouble at that time after the war and settled for a quiet life and Packie was never seen at a war commemorative event again, until he was in his eighties and no longer cared what people thought.

PACKIE AFTER THE WAR

Chapter Fifteen

A CIVILIAN LIFE

On returning to England after my recuperation at home, I was posted for a year to Catterbridge, on the Merseyside of Liverpool. The country was still on alert for a few years after the war, just in case Russia or anyone else had any great plans of world domination, so I had a year of peacetime service to complete. As a sign of respect for us veterans, the work assigned to us was not too difficult. This was a calm, yet lonely year, but it gave me time to reflect and mellow in a familiar and disciplined army routine. A return directly to civilian life at that time might have destroyed me as my head and body attempted to acclimatise to peacetime. Simple things, like walking down a street without alarm at every single noise about me, took some adjusting to. My relationship with food took time to normalise as well; although we still had war rationing, I found the abundance of a meal too good to be true and was inclined to conserve. I also found it more difficult to form close friendships at this time as I had no energy or interest in anything much except leaving the army and going home.

I endured the remainder of my service at Cheltenham by letting the humdrum of a routine working week and a tame English social life mellow and ease my buzzing heart and mind. Here we were prepared for Civvy Street, or civilian life and for getting a job. We had a good choice of careers in England and I was offered training and apprenticeships, but all I wanted was to return home to Ireland. In my anxiety, I wasted some great career opportunities at this time as my ambition and confidence played second fiddle to dreaming of an escape from the army. I was offered a career as a telephone engineer in Oxford, but I still refused. This may have been a sensible career opportunity, but I was so edgy and determined to be at home. At this point, I started playing my safety game of keeping my head down and my nose clean. I was never going to get trapped in any organisation again and from now on I was running solo. My final posting was to Victoria Barracks in Belfast before being demobbed from the Army in the summer of 1946. In theory, I was still on Reserve until the 23rd July 1951 and I prayed very hard for continuing peace.

I had been awarded the Star of Palestine, The Maltese George Cross, The African Star, The Defense Medal, The Greek Campaign Medal and The Star of Italy for my actions during the war. In England, and I suppose in most European and worldwide countries, I was considered a war hero. But it was nothing to brag about in Tyrone and that was the only place that mattered to me. And so it would be nearly sixty years later before I would actually wear those medals or accept any recognition. Before leaving the Belfast barracks, I was issued with new civilian clothing. This consisted of a pair of socks and shoes, a shirt, tie and trousers, a hat and underwear, along with a suitcase to carry it all. As I was leaving, I received my back-dated pay of many years, which had amounted to a small fortune in my young eyes. I bought my freedom, in the form of a motorbike, with that money. I was now twenty-five years old and mature beyond my years in many ways and, on the other hand, I was insecure and distracted. My army days were nearly over and now I had to make a life of my own. I packed my bag and headed home to Tyrone where I belonged. As I walked out through the gates of the barracks, I consciously stepped over a line in my head, leaving behind the army and that episode of my life. I had my army reference, but I knew that would count for nothing in the life I was returning to.

Patrick Mc Crystal Age 25
Military Conduct: Exemplary
An excellent type of regular soldier, who can turn his hands to most things. Has been a POW for 18 months. Smart, well turned out and alert he is absolutely reliable and has worked well. A dependable man and a hard and willing worker.

So that was the report on my 10 years of active service with the Army. The commanding officer who knew me best, Colonel French, was lying in a grave on Leros, so I was lucky to get a reference instead of a headstone inscription—many of my comrades received no words at all, just an unmarked grave somewhere in Europe. So there I was on my way back to Omagh, with no plan for the future. After following orders all those years I felt like a headless chicken, running on nervous, reserve energy. The thought of being home was my childish desire and the fact I was no longer a child did not matter to my parents or me, so long as I was home safe.

The family had moved to a house alongside the railway track between Beragh and Omagh. Despite the fact that this was an unfamiliar house to me it certainty felt like home. It was great to get to a dancehall, but the main source of entertainment was to ceili—visiting with the neighbours or having them call to your house. It was a time for telling stories, singing songs and playing games of cards and such. My brothers spent most of their time out working and socialising at night. Gerry was at home more and I got to know him better and for a few months the family always had Sunday together.

I signed on the dole, or unemployment register, and I was sent out to harvest corn and gather potatoes on local farms. It was amazing to discover the same lads who were on the dole when I left were still on it ten years later, and I was now in the same boat as they. We were all accepting the King's silver for being unemployed. I was sent from one dirty job to the next—so much for a heroes' welcome! I may have gained more respect for staying home on the dole and joining the IRA. Now there is a thought: what if I had chosen that path instead? I suspect I would have eventually ended up at the same point today, no matter which path I had chosen. My daughter would still have ended up murdered on that street in Omagh. Those bombers did not consider whose daughter was in that crowd or what political background they came from. The evil of revenge in their hearts just wanted blood and attention.

It did take time to settle down to a simple secure life on my return in 1946. The mindset hadn't changed much around home, but I was certainly thinking differently. Most people had never been further than Omagh, so my experiences and philosophies were just incomprehensible to my workmates. When I went searching for my army buddies, I found very few had returned home. Those of us who did kept in touch very little. We understood each other, but at home we lived in different communities, with different social cultures. I was back drifting from job to job, so I went to Scotland for a while to find work in a coalmine, but I could not cope with the small underground spaces so I moved on to England for work until I eventually arrived home in Beragh again for Christmas.

One night in early 1947, I was at a dance in St. Mary's Church Hall in Beragh and met a beautiful girl called Mary O' Donnell. She came from a townland called Mountjoy, away on the other side of Omagh, but she was working in a household in Beragh village at that time. Lucky for me I suppose, as it was love at first sight and it was easy for me to visit her in Beragh. She was the housekeeper for Conway's, the local drapers, who owned the only car in the village when I was at school. I was the first one ready for Mass every Sunday morning in my rush to get to Beragh in case I would see Mary. She was the only thing I was sure about. Otherwise, I was quite unsettled during my first years at home and had no idea what career path to follow. As an Army Reservist I was offered training for many different professions and I had job offers, but I was afraid of long-term commitment or using my army record for a reference.

So I took the difficult route for a few years, starting with a job in the local Nestlé milk factory for a year, until I decided I hated it. In the meantime, I was totally distracted from work anyway as Mary and I married on the fourth of February 1948, within a year of meeting each other. The ceremony was in Knockmoyle Chapel and then we went for dinner in the Royal Arms Hotel in Omagh. We had one night of a honeymoon in a hotel in Ballybofey, just across the border, twenty-five miles away. I had no difficulty making the decision to marry Mary O'Donnell, but it must have been a leap of faith for her parents. But they seemed to like me, as at first we moved into the farm with Mary's parents in Mountjoy.

When the factory work finally got to me, I decided to take up training for a trade. So I left Mary to go to Coleraine, about seventy miles away, for six months to train as a plasterer. Mammy said I should be good at it after all the mud plastering practice I had acquired as a child. On my return home, I was lucky enough to get a job with a local builder named McGuigan and I became a plasterer. Mammy died in 1950 and thankfully I was home before she passed away. The last thing my mother told me, on her deathbed, was that the Gypsy lady had also told her that her son, Packie would lose a child in horrible circumstances and she felt she needed to tell me. I don't think I passed much remark on that revelation, as I had no children at the time, so it was soon forgotten.

OUR WEDDING DAY

After Mammy died, three of my brothers moved away to England to look for work leaving only Peter and young Gerry at home with Daddy. Mary had our first daughter Rosemary in 1951 while we were still living in Mountjoy. It was a blessing, as she needed the support of her own mother due to a difficult birth and recovery. I had my motorbike to go to work on as their farm was seven miles out of town, on the picturesque slopes of a mountain called Bessie Bell. Mary and I dreamed about a house of our own, but we struggled along for a while because my work was not steady. Mary's sister was married and living in central London and she sent word about good work opportunities there as Britain continued to rebuild after the war. So I decided to go to London and earn some money to give us a better start. Mary and Rosemary would be safe with her parents and I moved in with her sister, her husband and family in London. I got a good job in a furniture shop in the centre of the city and worked long hours. I transported furniture around the shop and warehouse and I worked six days a week. Sunday was my day to go to Mass and visit the sights of London. I loved Petticoat Lane market, as I could stand still at one end of it and simply let the crowd carry me up through the stalls. I saw the latest technology in the windows of the shops on Tottenham Court Road and dreamed of owning one of those new television gadgets some day soon.

Chapter Sixteen

LIFE IN A NORTHERN TOWN

London is an interesting city, but I was pining for home and my wee family most of the time. Eventually after two years, I agreed with Mary that it was time for me to come home and accept any job I could find. So I went back to plastering again for a few years and luckily we also got the offer of a house in a newly built housing estate on the Derry Road in Omagh, finally giving us the opportunity to set up our own little nest. When in the mid-fifties, I got another job offer from the Post Office, as a telephone engineer, I was not too foolish or proud to take it this time. The Post Office was a civil service organisation and every job was highly sought after, but an excellent Army reference was a great asset. This was exactly the same career I had refused in Oxford on leaving the army, but now I had it on my own home doorstep. This was a good job for a Catholic man in the 1950's. The pay was good, but more importantly; it was permanent and stable, ideal for raising a family. Our new home was conveniently situated in town, so I could walk to work and save money on transport and Mary was not isolated during the day with shops and neighbours nearby.

Four years after Rosemary, our baby daughter Geraldine was born and a year later, Kate came along. It was four more years before our little Patricia came into the world. Our family life was calm and the girls have wonderfully happy memories of growing up. From a life of living with only men, I went to a world and family dominated by women. The girls were all so different from each other. Rosemary was confident and wise, possibly from the experience of being an only child and living with her grandparents in her early years. Geraldine and Kate were reared together and both were full of fun and energy. They always had friends around or had places to go. Geraldine was very fashionable and glamorous and Kate more practical and tomboyish. One thing for sure, none of them were quiet and they filled the house with laughter. Patricia was our quiet gentle lamb, shy and very much the youngest, with three additional mothers in her sisters. As youngsters, they would all arrive into our bed to play and chat in the mornings, and when they were teenagers they would arrive in at night after a dance to tell us the details. I thanked God every night for the love that surrounded me and I asked for little else. When my father died in August 1956, my old family home in Beragh disappeared as Gerry moved to England and never returned. Peter lived in Omagh and Lizzie in Belfast, so my house became the new centre point for the family to visit and communicate with. The strong links with Beragh loosened, but I will forever consider myself a Beragh man.

My job had a fairly regular routine and I was around home most weekends and holidays. On a Friday evening, I arrived home from work and put the wages in the china teapot on the dresser for Mary. She gave me my pocket money and I allocated each of the girls their pocket money of 2/6(a half-crown) from my allowance. If their cousins from Dublin were staying, they got the same. Mary was a great manager and she

GERALDINE, MARY, ROSEMARY, KATE, PACKIE & PATRICIA

could make that wage go a long way. She was also a great cook and we never used tinned food in our house. I had lived on tinned food long enough and I would never look at corned beef again. While Mary ran the house, the girls and I always had our play money. We would go into the town on Saturday to buy their magazines and some sweets. It didn't take much money to do me I must say. I didn't even bother owning a car, simply because we lived in town and walked anywhere we needed to go or took the bike. Our house was very close to St. Lucia barracks, where I had started my army training all those years ago. In fact, as I walked past the gates every day, I looked at the young soldiers and thanked God they lived in peacetime.

During the fifties and sixties, Northern Ireland was a relatively peaceful place to reside, with the benefits of a good Health and Welfare Service. The Nationalist community certainty experienced disparity, but the call for Civil Rights was growing throughout the world and I believed it was only a matter of time before equality triumphed.

I drove the van at work, enabling me to see the countryside and practice driving on straight, level surfaces. It was a far cry from swerving about on the war-torn Maltese landscape. I just loved my work and the friendship of the lads. We had a gas cooker for the kettle, and the tea tasted just fine as we sat and chatted through our lunch breaks at the side of the road. As telephone engineers, our job was to install new lines and repair any faults within the counties of Tyrone and Fermanagh. Sometimes I took overtime work in the neighbouring counties during storms or for a large installation contract, but mostly I was home every evening. Each day was a new adventure with opportunities to meet new people. New installations brought great excitement to a whole community, never mind the actual household the telephone came to. People were very friendly and I was grateful to have a good job in my home environment within the warmth of a culture I understood. Every morning I walked into the town with my lunch box under my arm, clocked in, lifted my schedule, and loaded up my van. Mostly we worked in teams and the banter between the lads was always great craic. It was so liberating to drive out though the gates of Omagh Post Office in search of a new address, which could be just a mile away, or forty miles up a mountain. We had such fun finding some of the houses, especially in County Fermanagh where the locals ignored road names and simply used a townland as an address.

We Irish have a very distinct method of communication that has fascinated many comedians and writers over the years and I must admit our style and speed of speech must confuse strangers. A typical address we received from the boss in the morning at the post office might have read something like: 'Mrs. Owens, near Gortin.' Well now, Gortin could cover a ten square mile radius and you must remember the concept of a satellite navigation system was only a twinkle in some inventor's eye yet. We were running blind a lot of the time, but once in the general vicinity we could find most phone owners by following the overhead telephone cables. Then there was the customer's own directions on how to get to their house: "Now do you know Jim Tom's shed at the crossroads, well take the middle road there and keep going until you come to the road on the left. Now don't take that road 'cause my sister lives down there, but keep going until you see the white house with a black cat sleeping on the windowsill. My house is the next after the next house on the right."

These instructions were often further complicated by the nicknames used for families in the area. If there were multiple families in an area with the same surname, each family was given a nickname. For example John Maguire is called the Doctor because his grandfather played a doctor in a parish stage play over thirty years ago. The Post Office would send us out to find John Maguire and nobody in the area would know him. On asking numerous people for directions, we would be questioned and suggestions made such as, "sure if you boys brought the telephone to the house in the first place, you must know where it is now!!" Eventually someone would say: "Sure you must be looking for the doctor, as he is the only one with a telephone up that road. Now what would he be doin' with one of those contraptions can you tell me." As if these mind games were not enough of a challenge, there was the added suspicion of the border mentality. People living along the border knew how to look after their own interests and keep silent about their business and their neighbours. This can simply be summed up in the words "He who asks no questions is never told a lie". So I spent my working years connecting the rural houses of Tyrone and Fermanagh to the world of communication and learning how to ask the right questions to find the whereabouts of those houses.

Some evenings I drifted down town to the pub for a Guinness and a chat with my mates as I was now old enough to drink Irish stout! The lads from work got along great and we always had plenty to discuss, but I avoided the political debates. Socially I had fitted in well to the town community, especially considering I was a country lad. I played bowls, cards and darts in my local community centre and competitively around the country. The Omagh team was extremely witty and we laughed all the time, except when we were playing bowls of course as we took the competition very seriously. I was in a team with three other men named Paddy McDermott, Paddy Quinn and Tommy McCrory, so it didn't take a rocket scientist to figure out which community we belonged to. When we went to play the British Legion team, I never let on I had quietly remained a member but was signed up from England and not the local branch. Our community group was part of the parish and we had a hall in the same building as the Order of Malta, would you believe. I did not join the Order, but I did do my First Aid training as part of my work. Mary liked to go to the bingo with her sister, but I had no interest in it, so she ran on and I babysat those nights.

We lived in a housing estate with lots of young families and our house was always full of children. We had a large front door step so the children could sit around and use the step as a stage for concerts. They knew all the Irish ballads and the current pop hits they heard on the radio. I had to step over children to get into the house in the evening after work. On a Saturday morning, the girls would come in early and jump on the bed telling stories and singing songs. I taught them 'It's a long way to Tipperary', 'Pack up your troubles in your old kitbag' and 'We'll meet again', which were our soldier songs and they never questioned why I knew them. The girls knew if they sang for me or massaged my hair they could sweet-talk me into any deal.

The first television broadcast in Northern Ireland was by the BBC in 1953. Ever since then I had been desperate to get a television so I saved my money for years. Two neighbouring houses got a television first, but I finally had saved enough money to go and invest in a television of our own. I came home with a push button black and white Bush television and the children in the whole park went mad. I had to put a huge aerial on the roof and soon we had pictures and sound. Now children were camped at our door in the hope of seeing a programme. Rosemary used to do deals with other children to get her homework done in return for a seat in our living room. For the children's programmes, the living room was standing room only, with additional faces pressed up against the windowpane outside. It was very funny to watch the amazed faces and the first film we watched was Wagon Train. On special occasions, everyone came to our home to watch things like the Grand National horse race or the All Ireland GAA football final. The house was often full with visitors playing cards and chatting in the kitchen and the children in the living room playing games or watching a film.

On a Sunday evening the television stations in Northern Ireland went off air for a few hours for the Protestants to go to church so I always made chips (french fries) for the girls at that time and, of course, all their friends arrived too. I'd grab the tea towel and tuck it over my trousers as an apron to start peeling the spuds and like magic children would appear from nowhere to stand at our hedge calling "can I have some chips Mr. Sisha?" I got that silly name, as the young ones couldn't pronounce our Patricia's name correctly, so if she was Sisha I must be Mr. Sisha. I ended up making chips all evening. So that was the life I was more than contented to settle into. As the years went by, I separated myself completely from the past and the horrors of war. Our children dominated our world and I enjoyed my work. It may have been a simple life but it was quite busy, enabling the years to roll by quickly. The girls spent their summers up and down to Dublin as they had many cousins down there, or the cousins came to us.

As teenagers, the girls were always coming or going somewhere. They all had jobs either babysitting or serving tables at the Royal Arms Hotel. With only one wage coming in our door, the girls needed these jobs for some independence and they all worked hard. Many a night they would arrive home with a crowd in tow wanting to play music. I had bought them a radiogram for playing their records and they loved it. Our house was a noisy place in those days with Mary and I relegated to the kitchen due to the teenage invasion. The young crowd learned to dance in our sitting room. The girls had lovely friends from all backgrounds, just good kids wanting to share the interests of youth. Curiosity got the better of me a number of times and I would pass by the room and see them all jiving. Many of them learned to jive with the swinging door by holding the handle. Geraldine was always jiving with the door. If order needed to be called I usually left Mary to the dirty work, except for one time I spoke to Rosemary when I was annoyed at her arriving home with her ears pierced. She immediately referred to the tattoos on my arms and I was shocked as I had always tried to keep them covered and had no defense for my argument. I regretted getting those tattoos most of my adult life as I could not roll up my sleeves to work or go to the beach.

Generally, the social and political problems in the Six Counties had not improved in the years following the world war. Tensions continued to simmer under the surface and understandably, parents found it difficult to keep the youth out of trouble in areas of high unemployment and social deprivation. Throughout the Sixties, young Catholics and entire families had continued to leave to find work in England, America and even Australia. Most of our educated young people left and, on finding the rest of the world appreciated their talents and enabled them to prosper regardless of their religion; they just never came back home. My family lived within a Nationalist community, but I had a job and a house when not everyone had that luxury. Omagh was not the worst place to live in, with some factories, government offices, two hospitals and the Army Camp boosting the service economy and providing some employment opportunities, yet many of the youth around our area left for foreign shores.

My babies had grown up in a blink of an eye and my girls were flying the nest. Rosemary met a young lad at a dance at the Irish Forester's Hall, or INF, and didn't tell us about him at first. But not much goes past my notice so I asked one of the doormen to point him out to me in the pub one night and I bought him a beer. When Rosemary finally brought Peter home as her future husband, they thought it an amazing coincidence that I had randomly offered him a drink some months before. I never put them past their innocent notion. She married in 1971 when she was nineteen years old and settled in England. Kate and

Geraldine went across the border to work in Dublin for a while but eventually they would come back home to settle down in Omagh. They all loved coming home to us, eventually bringing husbands and grandchildren with them.

We knew nothing about holidays except when we went to see the girls or family in Dublin. Sometimes we convinced Mary to visit Rosemary in England as she was homesick and could not afford a ticket home in the early days. I remember one time in the early seventies Mary, Patricia and I decided to go over to England for St. Patrick's Day, accompanied by a 23lb turkey for the dinner. Of course the turkey had to be searched by the security forces at the checkpoints, but we were well accustomed to that sort of hassle. Peter and Rosemary had just bought their first car, a VW Beetle, and excitedly came to meet us off the old cattle boat at Haysham. The five of us barely squeezed into the car and the front bonnet had to be tied closed with my shoelace to accommodate the overgrown turkey. We then proceeded to drive nearly three hundred miles in freezing fog to the centre of London to spend St. Patrick's Day with Mary's sister Tess. I won't even tell you the story about getting the enormous turkey into the oven, but it was great fun. We spent the remaining days viewing the sights of London as if I had never seen them all before. My life may have been simple, but it was peaceful and full of love. As long as I could sit with my back to the wall and keep a sharp lookout in front I was content. I was alert to every little detail in my environment and I tended to stay in familiar environments as much as possible no matter how curious I became.

Chapter Seventeen

WAR KNOCKS AGAIN

By 1969 the call for Civil Rights was strong across the world. Martin Luther King had been murdered the year before in America because of his non-violent campaign calling for civil rights for Black Americans and all poor citizens. Bob Dylan was singing that 'The times they are a changin' and the first humans had walked on the moon. In the North of Ireland the voice for change, especially among the student population, was also growing in strength. Peaceful demonstrations for equal rights sparked angry attacks from the Loyalists and by summer with the arrival of the annual marching season everything had spiraled out of control. On the 14th August British troops were deployed in the City of Derry to stop the rioting. But that night rioters rampaged through the Catholic districts of Belfast burning houses and attacking innocent people. On the 15th of August, the British Army arrived in force to restore order and protect the Catholic population. Calm returned but all those simmering tensions were now boiling in the blood of both communities and the Army remained. It was like Palestine in 1938. Even though there were promises of reform from Government and voices of reason calling for calm within both communities, a line had been drawn in the sand on that day and war was about to begin. It was a war that was to last for the next thirty or more years.

However in 1969 we did not know that was our future. Instead, we were optimistic that change was on its way. But by August 1971 there was no middle ground left and barricades, barbed wire fences and social segregation reinforced the line in the sand. In the next five months, one hundred and forty-three people lost their lives in bombings and shootings. The numbers and resolve of both armies swelled. No matter who is right or who is wrong, no matter which side you affiliate to, I knew from experience that freedom costs too many innocent lives on all sides. All I could see was the bodies of those women and children of Dresden. Why does freedom always have to be bought the hard way? I thought that fate surely could not deal me another hand of war, but it had, and I was forced to make the best of it. I was born an Irishman, but grew up and lived my life as a British citizen just like millions of Irish in England. In countries all over the world people carry their Irish citizenship in their heart. Northern Ireland citizens could hold both Irish and British passports and live within their affiliated culture with relative ease. Granted, there were problems, but whether I liked it or not, my home was in a British state and 'when in Rome, do as the Romans do' seemed the smartest strategy to live by. Within that state I was also living deep in the heart of a Nationalist community so my life was predominately Irish in culture, which was confusing enough to create a conflict in anyone's psyche. In this war I was a civilian and I had choices, unlike when I was a soldier. I suppose I could have moved the family to England. I am sure I could have got a transfer with the Post Office but it is difficult to move teenagers from a culture they understand. We could have moved south, across the border, as other family members had, but Tyrone was home and I had lived in exile long enough and I just wanted to be home.

Anyway, what peace could I have found anywhere in the world while family and friends were here? So I decided to stay. Generally, those years were not so difficult really. Of course there were body searches going into shops and public places, roadblocks with the questions about where you were coming from and where you were going now. My name identified me very much as of the Nationalist and Catholic community and little could those young British soldiers imagine that I was once in similar shoes to them, as a teenager, on a lonely road at night, holding a gun in a strange land—the only difference being that I had been attempting to decipher between Jews and Arabs in the Holy Land. It scares me to think how naive I must have been back then, at the tender age of eighteen. Life had many profound lessons to teach me in the subsequent years.

In the thirty years of conflict, Omagh town had suffered few deaths during the troubles other than five British Army soldiers killed in an IRA booby-trap car bomb at Knock-na-Moe Castle Hotel on the17 May 1973. The hotel was a popular nightspot for most of the local young people, including my own girls, and it was a miracle more young lives had not been lost in that attack. Around the same time, four IRA men lost their lives on the Gortin Road when the car bomb they were transporting into Omagh blew up. Otherwise, despite the fact that we had multiple bombs in town, I think only one other person had died, but many security force and paramilitary lives had been lost in shootings and explosions on the country roads surrounding the town. We lived with a military presence and we all adjusted as best we could to it. The girls managed to lead a normal social life and get home safe every night, but I did worry when they went to nightclubs out of town or across the border to Monaghan or Donegal, as I knew how nervous those young soldiers were on the border checkpoints in the dark. Also, there was the ever-present risk of firebomb attacks or shootings at hotels and nightclubs in the North, but young people needed to socialise and we let them run on with their friends. When Geraldine had been thrown into the hedge by the bomb that time, I became very edgy and protective, but I did not run.

Maybe I should have moved the family out of here, but then again, I could not move Mary away from her large extended family and the girls away from their friends. After Rosemary married she spent many years abroad and in fact one of our grandsons was born in Hong Kong so I guess he is actually Chinese in a way, but I never went to visit her there. I was curious about the Far East as I had been assigned there in 1945 but miraculously that assignment eluded me. Like my Uncle Patrick, I loved to hear and talk about the world, but I could not admit I had seen it with my own two eyes. I had amazing stories to tell in my head, but I had no voice to share them. As years passed, the girls returned from foreign holidays with stories of wonderful places saying "Daddy, you could not believe how beautiful the weather is in Greece" or whatever country they had been to. I simply listened with great interest, but I could not bring myself to say I had seen it all before. Oh, how I missed that brilliant Mediterranean sunshine heating my bones and the cosmopolitan atmosphere of the Valletta nightlife. No, I had no right to think of such things, as I had all I needed right here in my safe family home in Omagh.

When I was a prisoner, I had had time to dream of the life I wanted back home and I painted pictures in my head of a future after the war. These dreams were about the very basics of living, like having shoes in high shine or owning my own shaving razor or a suit of clothes and having a cupboard full of food. I think that once my life was secure, I was afraid to ask for anything more luxurious. Another one of those dreams was of my own garden with food readily available to me. It seemed a simple enough request—what difference did it make to me what government ran the country, as long as they left me in peace and I had food for the table. Nothing is ever perfect, and I knew things could be a hell of a lot worse. I also knew kicking, screaming and throwing stones like a spoiled child is pointless against a powerful adversary. Unless you have a bigger stick, it is advisable to co-operate and negotiate. So many countries in Europe became absorbed within foreign borders during and after the war, but their people still held their identity in their souls. They waited quietly, and when libration came they still had their national pride. They had not lost respect by lashing out at their own people. Here in Ireland, the idealisms of the warlords on both sides continued to drive our youth from our shores, to places where they could truly celebrate being Irish. There are millions of people living all over the world who still consider themselves Irish, wherever they reside, as our culture runs very deep in our veins, deeper than any border or governing power could influence or understand. Being Irish is in our soul, our songs, our dance, our folklore and customs. Being Irish is about our personality and ability to forge new friendships anywhere we go and it is about our passion for justice and compassion for the underdog, no matter what government we find ourselves living under. If we listen, we can hear our ancestors plea to look for an Irish nation based on intelligence, respect and justice, not on ignorance, revenge and bigotry. Maybe our Tir Na nOg is really the unique Irish culture we carry in our souls, lived out in a global community. Maybe St. Patrick should come back and drive out the innocent this time and leave the island to the snakes to fight it out.

I could have lived anywhere as I love people and languages came easy to my ear. I was not afraid of hard work and I was extremely adaptable. Yes, I was an ideal candidate for a foreign national, but I did not leave Tyrone. I could not uproot my life. We marked my retirement from the Post Office in 1984 by moving house to a newly built bungalow on the outskirts of town. This move gave me a bigger garden with space for my long wished-for greenhouse and my own tomatoes. As a child, I had loved the marking of the seasons with the planting and harvesting of the potato crop and other vegetables in Mammy's garden. As I marched through Malta and Palestine it had been amazing to behold the vivid colours of tomatoes, peppers and exotic fruits growing lazily in the sunshine. Yes, I had always wanted a garden of my own and, although my garden in Omagh was small, it was utilized to the maximum. It turned out I was as green fingered as my mother. I had no bother filling my day between the garden, the family and the community centre. The front garden was for the roses—all different colours and varieties to signify diversity. In all their beautiful colours they lived in prefect harmony, blooming in all their glory during the summer months. Individually each bloom was special but all together they were magnificent.

Humans are very adaptable really and we continued with a normal life as we thought. Life wasn't that bad. But the years rolled on and the troubles got worse and the hatreds got deeper with hunger strike deaths, bombings and political words of venom. It was like a slow moving nightmare and before I realised, I had grandchildren heading out into that world. All of Europe had lived through worse conditions, during and after the war, as they endured invasions and border movements in their countries, but they were now at peace. Even the Berlin wall came down in 1989 and the Eastern European countries found their feet again relatively peacefully. What was wrong in Northern Ireland? Borders seem to sort themselves out after time everywhere else, but here we just didn't have patience to wait. Revengeful attacking just strengthened the border and the resolve to keep it. We were in a state of bully-boy rule on all sides and the peace-loving middle ground had no voice. Eventually we hoped voices of reason and compromise would win through. And so they did, coming from the grassroots up. Ordinary people made community efforts to understand each other and assert their right to peace. From among the bullies, a few compromising political voices spoke of stretching out a hand of peace and offering dialogue instead of exclusion, revenge and bitterness. Over many years, these voices attracted American, British and Irish government leaders to speak a language of compromise regarding Northern Ireland and a solution was a possibility. My family knew how to keep out of trouble and if we kept our heads down and our noses clean we could manage through the remainder of this conflict. And so we did, right through all those years to the bitter end, as we thought. I'd forgotten about the dying kicks of war. My daughter was killed after the war was supposedly declared over and when the community had dropped its guard.

WITH OUR GIRLS

OUR GRANDCHILDREN

Chapter Eighteen

SURVIVING 1998

On Sunday morning, the day after the Omagh Bomb, Mass was held in our local Catholic parish. The priest prayed for Geraldine Breslin, a young parishioner, who had died in hospital during the night. Geraldine was one of the first to be identified and named and many other names were to be added to that list, not only in our parish, but in many other parishes, some as far away as Spain. The congregation in Omagh sat with their heads in their hands, some crying and most completely numb with shock. The priest told them: "From the point of view of the people who suffered there was no distinction, Catholic and Protestant, young and old, there was no question of wanting to get one side rather than another. The whole thing sounds so terrible, so stupid, so foolish, and so senseless".

During the days of the wake, Geraldine's husband Mark told us he had been allowed a brief visit to see Geraldine in Intensive Care in Omagh before she left for Belfast. She was semi-conscious, her head, an eye and her face were bandaged, but she managed to mutter, "I'm sorry". Mark could not stay long as the doctors were concerned about internal bleeding and it was decided to transfer her by helicopter to a specialist unit in Belfast. When Mark got to Belfast a few hours later in the car, she had already died. He sat with her body for half an hour, just holding her hand, before he came home to tell her son that his mother was dead. As people came to the wake house, they brought accounts of the events in Omagh and of seeing Geraldine in the moments before the blast. It was difficult to hear all the little bits of information coming in, but I wanted to hear everything to help build up a complete picture of Geraldine's last day in my mind.

On Thursday morning we had to let Geraldine's coffin go from her family home. It is strange that, as parents, we always picture our kids as little ones no matter how old they get. I could picture Geraldine sleeping in the cot or jumping on our bed on a Christmas morning. At the funeral mass the priest who married Geraldine and Mark spoke about her life describing her as "A beautiful woman who was the salt of the earth". He went on to speak about how "the callousness of planting a bomb and surrounding it with as many people as possible, defies all belief, all understanding and all reason". But he also went on to offer a positive word by saying, "The blackness of evil lay heavy over our town, but in this blackness, lights begin to shine. People reached out and helped the injured, gave hope to the dying and held the dead. And this goodness, which was such a challenge to evil, gave us back the gift of hope".

It is just a shame that humans have to push things to the very edge of darkness before they can see the light. Why can't they reach out to understand each other before such deeds are considered? I have to admit that at this time I was struggling to recognise any sign of hope in the distance. I had so many questions and doubts and I needed to understand. I knew we might never hear the truth about the politics behind this bombing and there was no logical or moral justification that either side could offer in their defence to explain why anyone could believe in any cause that justified this sacrifice of innocent life. Each man, woman, child and baby on that street just wanted to live in peace and build a future of hope. But just like Hitler, these evil men wanted their ideal world and vengeance, no matter who had to be annihilated in the process. Had Ireland not learned enough about bullying through the centuries to understand that hatred and revenge begets more hatred and revenge? No side is free from blame in a tit-for-tat war. I remembered all those thousands of bodies I had witnessed in Europe during the war and thought, my little girl was now like them, an innocent victim of mindless, random revenge.

As a soldier, I had stood up to being considered a target, but my daughter definitely had not. A bomb does not have the intellect to discriminate and judge who is to be sacrificed, so once the powerful leaders of any army give the order to attack, it is certain that everyone is fair game. But the consequences of war and suffering lay far from the eyes of the powerful decision makers. But I understood the role of a soldier very well — when an order comes down you must carry it out. There is little moral choice or intellectual reasoning. The soldier is trapped between taking an order to take another life, or sacrificing his own. So who is responsible for the murder? Who should take responsibility when the line between self-defence and revengeful slaughter is crossed? I had lived under the rain of fire in Malta as Italy and Germany revengefully attempted to annihilate the Maltese population for not surrendering. In Dresden, it was the American and British who deliberately taught Germany a lesson by targeting a defenceless civilian population. Both the Dresden and Omagh bombings were executed at the end of a war, when the enemy was practically defeated. These attacks were not the dying kicks of a wounded animal, but the winners giving the general population a good kicking when they were already down, to make sure they understood who won. The young lads with their fingers on the trigger in all armies will have to deal with the moral questions and guilt of their individual actions when they are mature enough to understand what they were ordered to do, whether they are in prison or free. But what of the warlords, the ones who go on to gain political and financial advantage and do not even recognise their guilt? It is very easy to incite revengeful emotions with talk of historical wrongs, but talk of history can be warped if done without experiencing that history's suffering. I am reminded of my grandparents who lived through the famine, the Irish uprising and the civil war. They knew that revengeful talk would only bring the same suffering to their descendants, so they disengaged from the emotions to protect us and hoped for better times. Other parents, on all sides, burdened their children with the emotional pain of history and hoped for vengeance thus the warlords found their foot soldiers already impassioned. I could now understand my parents' despair at my decision to join the army, to become a pawn in the big boys' game of war, but I also knew from my own experience that armies are needed for protection and that without them the bullies will find their way to our doorstep. The problem is that an Army, fueled on anger and revenge, becomes a bully itself. So in Ireland we got years of misery, as all sides indiscriminately endeavored to settle old scores. Neither side cared about the people on an Omagh street, or any other street for that matter. They were just a consequence of the battle. They had innocently got caught in the crossfire. With all my experience of war, I let this happen to my family and that is what bothered me the most. I should not have underestimated the brutality of evil men, for I knew better. I had dropped my guard before the battle was over.

The months that followed the Bomb were just so difficult. Anger bubbled under my cool surface as I tried to get a grip of my grief for Geraldine. I blamed myself for not protecting her, for not warning her and for not going to her immediately. When I wasn't angry with myself I was angry with the perpetrators. Whoever carried out this cowardly deed needed to feel this pain. This was my country, just as much as theirs. I held an Irish passport, but fought a war as a British citizen to protect our culture. Generations of my family had survived on this island and I had a right to raise my family here. How dare they invade our lives like this? These faceless evil men deserved no respect and I only wished they could understand the pain they had caused. I asked God the big question of why. Why did he let this happen to me? I had never asked for wealth or power and I had devoted my life to my family, my Church and my community. I tormented my head searching for a reason for my punishment. But anger was not my natural temperament and slowly my heart softened.

The weeks and months after the bomb were a very bizarre time for many of the bereaved and injured families of Omagh. We continued to be tortured for a few years by hoax bomb alerts from anonymous phone calls. These calls caused panic and destroyed any town trading as, with each call, the town centre had to be evacuated, driving shoppers away from Omagh and traumatising the many injured who were attempting a return to work in town.

The world press milled around and dignitaries flew in from around the globe. Visitors to our town included President Clinton and Hilary Clinton, Tony and Cheri Blair, Prince Charles and the Queen, Mary McAleese, President of Ireland, local politicians and dignitaries from Spain. As a family, we were invited to meet some amazing people and experience events we would not have ordinarily been part of. Just like my nights under the pyramids, during the war, I think I might have appreciated the privilege of these events if it were not for the circumstances that brought me there. I hoped I was shaking hands with powerful people who believed in truth and justice, but I was unsure who my faceless enemy truly was. I did warm to the Clinton family and they had great respect and time for us as a family. On a later visit they brought their daughter Chelsea to meet us in Omagh and we had great fun with them. Bill was speaking with me and he called over to Chelsea saying, "Come over here Chelsea and meet a real Paddy". We all had a great laugh. I also had a great day at the President of Ireland's House, Áras an Uachtaráin in Dublin. The President, Mary McAleese insisted I sat beside her and we had a chat. We were treated like royalty and I tasted my first caviar. I could get accustomed to fine dining all right, but it could not take away my pain.

PACKIE, MARY & KATE WITH PRESIDENT CLINTON

Good people came to remind us that there are more angels than demons in the world. The St. Vincent De Paul quietly brought funds to our house to assist with the additional bills at the time. People called and events were organised to pull us out of the house, even U2 sent VIP concert tickets to my granddaughters. The wonderful people at the WAVE Trauma Centre came into our lives with shared understanding of being bereaved or traumatised through violence in Northern Ireland. Mary found great comfort at WAVE as she could voice feelings there with others who had also suffered, feelings that were too difficult to voice at home. She often said she wanted to forgive the bombers because she could not die in peace until she did. Mary told us "I admire people who say they forgive, but how can I forgive faceless people. I need to look them in the eye to forgive". I suppose I had been dealing with faceless foes for much longer and knew that this world of ours very rarely satisfies us with truth and justice. What I did know is that, in the pursuit of both, we run the risk of letting the frustration lead us to anger and resentment. I also knew that the guilty cannot find peace by remaining faceless as their need for forgiveness will eventually drive them mad. In Omagh we had no faces to forgive, so the best we could do was hand the justice issue over to a greater power, be that in heaven or less likely on earth, and protect our own souls from hatred.

With time, the house regained some laughter as we all realised the children had a right to a happy life and we could not let our past ruin their future. The first two years were a nightmare and we survived them with the distractions of official visits and forming a structured community group to lobby for our needs as victims and to plead for justice and peace. The families named it "The Omagh Support & Self Help Group". Our mission is to campaign for the human rights of all victims of terrorism. As a collective group we could go out into the world and meet as many people as possible that might influence our leaders to talk peace. This work kept us focused and challenged through the early Millennium years and still our work is not finished in 2010 as we still search for the elusive truth.

Famous people came together to make a CD called, "Across the Bridge of Hope" for Omagh. These wonderful, generous people thought of our suffering and gave us their healing voices of comfort. Liam Neeson recited a Seamus Heaney poem; Sinead O' Connor, The Divine Comedy, Boyzone, The Corrs, Daniel O' Donnell, Van Morrison, Ash, U2, local girl Juliet Turner, Paul Brady, Omagh Community Choir and Enya all contributed beautiful songs. Our Geraldine would have been delighted with such a talented line up to sing for her as she loved music. Patricia and Mary had always watched the Late Late Show, broadcast from RTE in Dublin, and they got the chance to attend the live show on a special night devoted to Omagh just before Christmas 1998. Appearing on the Programme were U2, The Corrs, Brian Kennedy and Paul Brady. Noel Gallagher of Oasis sent a message to the audience, made up of people from Omagh and Buncrana, who had been traumatised by the bombing. I was particularly taken by Bob Geldof's reading of a WB Yeats poem, 'The Second Coming'.

> *"Things fall apart; the centre cannot hold;*
> *Mere anarchy is loosed upon the world;*

> *The blood-dimmed tide is loosed, and everywhere*
> *The ceremony of innocence is drowned;*
> *The best lack all conviction, while the worst*
> *Are full of passionate intensity."*

I could hear Yeats telling me that the peacemakers lack conviction, while the bullies have all the passion. That is why evil has been winning the battle thus far. If only the voices of compassion, understanding and peace could assert themselves with 'passionate intensity' as Yeats puts it, then we could yet win the war against the bullies. I could see how my old strategy of keeping the head down and the nose clean was not enough to keep the peace.

I knew our town had a real responsibility to send out a clear message of love and peace, but also to show that we victims had the backbone to stand up for truth and justice in a world of sweet talking politicians and bloodthirsty madmen on all sides. As the years rolled by we listened to all the promises of justice and hoped that no community would suffer like us again, but as I watched the twin towers fall in New York in 2001 and I listened to the irresponsible and revengeful reactions to that evil deed, I realised that no-one had learned from us at all. In 2003, I lay in bed night after night listening to the drone of high-level American bombers passing overhead on their flight path to Iraq and I felt the earth shake in my soul. I could see the devastation they intended to create. I could see the bodies of men, women and children and maybe whole families at a time in the bottom of mass graves. Could the sacrifice of thousands of these unprotected innocent lives in the poor homes of Iraq really bring back the beautiful lives lost in New York? Would the loss of thousands of young American and British soldiers make the underlying problem go away. Could they not see that evil had thrown them the bait of hatred and was just waiting for their retribution? Had humankind not found another way to resolve conflict other than randomly killing innocent babies and children?

With every winner comes a defeated loser who is angry and eventually eager for revenge, whether in that lifetime or by ensuring that a vendetta is past down to the next generations. Therefore, if we use emotions instead of intelligence to correct the wrongs of the past we will never get off the roundabout of revenge and war. Of course, evil comes and the bullies will rise, so we will need to protect ourselves—armies are necessary for defence and protection, but an army must be very disciplined and be led by intelligence, not emotions. Orders are easily given from an ivory tower and impossible to refuse in the muddy trenches, so an army is only as good as its commanders. Most young soldiers in any army only want to do some good, but often in the thick and confusion of the battle, the ends might seem to justify any means. Young people need to hear the intimate story of the individual suffering of war, instead of always getting the satellite view about vengeful heroes and one-sided victory. I was reminded of a quote I read years ago, when I was searching for an explanation as to how ordinary people had allowed and enabled the atrocities during the Second World War to happen under their noses. It bothered me that soldiers carried out orders to gas children to death. Would I have carried out an order like that or dropped a bomb on a playground if under orders to do so? How do good people let these things happen?

> *"The only thing necessary*
> *for the triumph of evil*
> *is for good men to do nothing"*

It is unknown who said this though it was thought to have been Edmund Burke (1729-1797) but he never published it. Fear can silence most good people no matter how much they disagree, especially if they are protecting a family. Maintaining the status quo is much easier than martyrdom.

Another problem is that all sides think they are justified and right, with their God on their side, but I say that nothing justifies taking innocent, unprotected and precious life. Soldiers should face soldiers and protect the innocent and I thank God that I was never in a position that demanded otherwise.

In Omagh, we did not know exactly who the enemy was and although we demanded the truth, we did not ask for more blood. I still like to think that Omagh contributed some positive message to the world and that has kept me going through those difficult years and we continue to reach out a hand of compassion and understanding to victims everywhere.

Chapter Nineteen

FACTS REVEALED

About a year after Geraldine died, we got a phone call from a woman asking if her teenage son could come to see us. She said he needed to talk to us about something important. The young lad was very upset at meeting us, as he introduced himself, as the mystery lad who had stayed with Geraldine on the street and held her hand on the journey to the hospital. This lad was only a teenager, who had suffered so badly over the past year due to the trauma he had witnessed. Thank God he came to us to answer our questions and release himself from his nightmare. As he told us about his time with Geraldine he calmed down. He said that she had cried out for Mark as she lay in the rumble. This young lad came to her and held her hand as she cried and they waited for help together. I had to close my eyes and turn away from the vivid images of such a scene. I don't know if I cried for him, or my own traumatic youth, but I cried. My heart broke for the innocent boy who was destroyed that day, but I also thanked God he had been transformed into an angel to hold the hand of my distraught daughter. Evil cannot conquer a compassionate soul, as evil does not understand the concept of compassion and love. That evening we all cried together and that special lad walked out of our home ready to face life again. He could sleep again as he finally let his burden go and went on to make a good life in Australia I believe.

The inquest, two years later in September 2000, finally answered a few more of our questions. The venue was the Omagh Leisure Centre, which had also been the Incident Centre where many families had waited for news of loved ones in the days after the explosion. I am sure it was difficult for them to return to that building. We were very anxious about attending the inquest, but we sat through it all to hear the coroner, Mr. Leckey's report about the cause of death in each case. It was just heart-breaking for everyone concerned. Then, it was our turn, as I heard my daughter's name read out and the coroner stated his findings:

"Geraldine Breslin, another of the assistants from Watterson's, died eight hours after the bomb, having been transferred to Belfast. Mrs. Breslin, a 43-year-old mother, was suffering from horrendous multiple injuries and severe internal bleeding, it was remarkable she survived so long. She appeared to be a woman "fighting very much to live".

So now I had most of the jigsaw pieces in place to reveal Geraldine's last day on this earth. It was a sad picture to face and despite the fact that we still had not found the nurse from the helicopter it brought some closure to my questions and a chance to start a grieving process.

As the months rolled into years, we got on with the job of living. The grandchildren were graduating and finding careers and partners and there was so much to celebrate. Then our first great granddaughter arrived and the world was full of light. I started to talk a little more about my war experiences to the family and Kate started taking notes of the dates and places I had been to during the war. I think I was surprised by their interest and their sense of pride about my history. We found some of my medals and I polished them up, while the family secretly ordered up any other medals owed to me from the Ministry of Defence. To my surprise, the Duchess of Abercorn arrived at my home to present the long overdue medals to me.

Remembrance Sunday is held every year in November, all around the world, for the soldiers killed during the world wars. Omagh has held a service at the Cenotaph in town every year since the war ended, but I had never attended, as it was not the place for a Catholic to be seen. Also, I had no intention of taking a risk to attend, after eleven civilians had been killed in a bombing at the war memorial in the neighbouring town of Enniskillen, during a WW1/WW2 Remembrance Day ceremony in November 1987. The attack became known as the "Poppy Day Massacre." But in 2004, our Kate decided it was time I went to commemorate my service and remember my fallen comrades. I was not sure about such an outing as I had no idea what happened at such an event and people might laugh at wee Paddy walking in the door.

When the morning arrived, Kate kept pushing and I eventually put on my coat and got ready to go. Kate had sown my seven medals together on a lapel pin. She pinned it on my left chest, over my heart and I immediately covered them up with my coat. I felt so self-conscious about them, as I had never sported my medals before and, at eighty-four years of age, it seemed ridiculous to start now. I was due more unclaimed medals, but after all these years a fee was charged so I didn't bother to get them. Anyway, I didn't need more weight, as my left shoulder might droop and spoil my otherwise straight posture. I was nervous and nearly had the coat off again, only Kate is very bossy when she is determined, so I had no choice but go to town with her.

When we arrived at the venue, I recognised some of the faces from around the town. These men had always held their heads high about their army service, but they knew nothing about Wee Paddy's contribution. Most were Protestant men who had served here during the Troubles or had a few tours of duty abroad during peacetime. To my disappointment none of my mates from 1939 were still around to stand with me. I had secretly hoped somebody might be there that day. As we walked up the aisle, I could see some heads turning and eyes rising in wonderment about what I was doing there. I was shy at first, but my confidence grew as the service continued. Then I took a sudden notion that I was as good as anyone in the room, so I threw off my coat and revealed my medal collection. It must have shocked a few people as after the prayers, I was questioned about where I had found the medals. One particular guy I knew around town wanted to know what battles I had been in. If these veterans were baffled by a Paddy in their midst, what would my own community think of a closeted British soldier in theirs? But I had finally stepped out to show my face and now everybody knew my truth. I have attended Remembrance events in the years since and I have no difficulty sporting my medals anymore. I have matured enough now to ignore negative comments and not to worry about whom it upsets. It was my history and I was proud of my contribution to the world.

SPORTING MY MEDALS FOR THE FIRST TIME IN 2004

By 2006, my wife Mary was unwell and, in addition my daughter Kate received a very negative cancer prognosis and was sent home from hospital with little hope one day in April. That evening, Rosemary and her husband in England impulsively jumped in the car and drove from their home in England to The Shine of Our Lady of Lourdes in the Pyrenees in southern France to ask for a cure. Our Lady appeared many times to a young girl called Bernadette in 1858 there. Approximately five million people visit the shrine every year looking for spiritual, emotional and physical healing. There have been sixty-seven medically and scientifically proven cures at Lourdes and many more unproven healings. On arriving, Rosemary and Peter slept and then went down to the Grotto for the candlelight parade. As they walked along in the huge, continuously flowing crowd of candleholders in the night procession, Rosemary noticed a group of people wearing 'Order of Malta' uniforms with Ireland on their badges. The Order attends the sick as nurses and helpers, the same as the St John or Red Cross. Anyway, Rosemary fell into conversation with one of the girls from Dublin called Wendy, who recognised Rosemary's Irish accent. Rosy explained she was from Omagh, but living in England for many years and of course Omagh always sparks the bomb discussion. Wendy explained that she had travelled to Lourdes with the Omagh branch and she would talk to them that night at the hostel. Rosemary told her about Geraldine and gradually they got separated in the crowd.

The next night, Rosy and Peter were standing on the bridge over the River Gave taking photographs when a man in the Order of Malta uniform walked past. Rosy and he immediately recognised each other as childhood next-door neighbours. As they talked, Wendy from Dublin came running up calling "She's here, she's here, she wants to meet you, can you believe that she is here". Rosemary asked, "What do you mean she's here?" With that another girl in uniform approached and said "My name is Joanna and I was the nurse from the Tyrone County Hospital who went with Geraldine in the helicopter that night. I am sorry I let her go on you, I am so sorry." They hugged and cried and walked along together, oblivious to the crowds. They held their candles, walking and talking and Peter still describes the moment the procession stopped and they stood right under the statue of Our Lady and St. Bernadette. How could they have found each other, so far from home and in the throng of so many people? Well only the Order of Malta uniform and the fact Wendy remembered Geraldine's name when she returned to the hostel, which caught Joanna's ear. God works in very mysterious ways I think. The next day the word from home was brighter, as a new doctor offered Kate new hope with an alternative treatment. A few weeks later, Joanna came to visit us at home. She told us that Geraldine had been conscious for some of the journey and she had asked for us. We told her how delighted we were to know such a lovely person was there when we could not. It must have been a nightmare in that helicopter, to experience flying under such circumstances. Geraldine did not die until Joanna had safety delivered her to Belfast. The final piece of the jigsaw slipped into place; we knew Geraldine had not been alone and both Mary and I got peace at last.

Four months later, in August 2006, my world was shook again, only this time in a gentle way. Mary had been ill in the previous year and by August she was home from hospital and with us to die. The girls helped me nurse her and those last days are precious in my memories. As we sat around talking, Mary told us that Geraldine was sitting on the bed with us and she was waiting for her. Just before she died, Mary asked for a priest and just as she spoke, he came through the door to her. Later, as we recited the Rosary prayer, Mary slipped silently away from us and I was alone for the first time in fifty-eight years.

Mary's death was natural and easier to accept than the brutal loss of life by unnatural causes. At first, I busied myself with the funeral arrangements and the family, but eventually I had to face my grief. Mary was my rock and she had saved me all those years ago. I relied on her practically and emotionally. Now at eighty-seven years of age, I had to test my own self-reliance. The garden still kept me busy, with all its chores throughout the year, I made my own dinner every day and the girls took me shopping or anywhere I needed to go. Kate and I went to Derry every week for her chemotherapy and often called on my sister Lizzie on the way home. My cousin, Noel Maguire, helped me with any extensive DIY jobs around the house and he enabled me to remain actively independent with my household maintenance. I continued to go on my holidays to Rosemary over in England

and my granddaughter and great granddaughter moved into my house, so that kept my spirit young and stopped me turning into a grumpy old man.

My days continued to be busy and I found a new way to live my life. Lately, my sister Mary Elizabeth reminded me again of our father's favourite song and for the first time I heard the words and realised they speak to me also. I suddenly understood my poor father, who still had young children to feed when he was sixty years old. Gerry was barely raised by the time he lost Mammy and died himself, just before reaching his seventieth birthday. No wonder he was serious and sensible, as he had lost so many loved ones, but without a close bond with his children, he did not welcome comfort like I had from my family. Hearing the words of that song after seventy years was surreal. I could imagine my daddy sitting there beside the gramophone and my mother singing along to "The Lament of The Irish Emigrant" as she moved around the kitchen.

Lament Of The Irish Emigrant.

The place is little changed, Mary,
The day is bright as then,
The lark's loud song is in my ear
And the corn is green again;
But I miss the soft clasp of your hand,
And your breath warm on my cheek,
And I still keep list'ning for the words
You never more can speak.

Yours was the good, brave heart, Mary,
That still kept hoping on,
When the trust in God had left my soul,
And my arm's young strength was gone:
There was comfort ever on your lip,
And the kind look on your brow-
I bless you, Mary, for that same,
Though can you hear me now?

> *I'm biddin' you a long farewell,*
> *My Mary—kind and true!*
> *But don't forget me, darling!*
> *In the land your goin' to;*
> *They say there's bread and work for all,*
> *And the sun shines always there—*
> *But you'll not forget old Ireland,*
> *And your wee Paddy there!*

How lonely my father must have felt in the years after my mother died as he lived out his last years in that house along the railway track. My brothers all left one by one for England with Gerry following in their footsteps just after Daddy died. Lizzie and I have always remained close and I go to see her often. She is ninety-two and still running her home and looking after her husband. Our other brothers, Dessie, Bernard, Francie and Peter had no family and are long since dead, but Gerry still lives in England. Lizzie and I really never knew him growing up as we were both gone from home by the time he was born, but now we keep in touch with him and his two children. My stepbrother Tony lived his life in Beragh and he had four daughters. My stepsister Gertie moved away to Belfast and then England to live closer to her two children. Her sister Annie remained a spinster and kept in close contact with my family until her death in 1994.

As executor of my sister's will I was granted the position of correcting a wrong within the family. Lizzie told me that before I left for Malta in 1937 Gertie had given birth to a son. Unable to keep him during those harsh times he was in the care of the Workhouse until she found him a good foster home. He was seven when she married, but by then he was settled and happy so she walked away and did not disturb his life again. I found her son and his family in 1995 to give him a small inheritance from his unknown aunt and, although sixty years too late, I welcomed him into our family. I explained his royal blood lineage from the ancient O'Neill kings and that he was named after his ancestor Owen Roe O'Neill. My father had told us about his first wife's genealogy and their role in Irish history. We found the O'Neill burial plot in Beragh with the family crest of the Red Hand of Ulster engraved above his relatives names. It is also sad to think that of my father's sixteen children, Owen is one of only four men carrying the McCrystal name into the future and daddy never knew him. My childhood home is long since gone and the only traces of my family in Beragh now are a few McCrystal and McGinn names inscribed on headstones in a lonely graveyard.

The next few years continued with my usual recovery strategy of continuing to breathe and keeping very busy in the garden. Geraldine's son grew into a fine young man and no longer needed my care. I was still fast on my feet and always ready for action when anyone was going somewhere. Until the age of ninety-one, I spent many of my days in the garden, still making jam and my greenhouse was full of tomatoes. The potato crop still marked the seasons and I could dig most of my own dinner fresh from my own garden. I like to cook, and the cupboards are always full of food, just in case of an emergency, but you still will never see corned beef on the menu in my kitchen. The family kept me occupied and interested in modern things and when my granddaughter, Kerry-Ann, moved to Australia I communicated with her over the Internet.

If only I was seventeen again and knew about Australia and had all the choices of this 21st century.

For the first time I had the freedom to speak in earnest about my life and when I recognised a kindred spirit in my newly found grand-niece Mary, I did not hesitate in asking her to write my story. Of course she had little experience with writing, but I knew she understood my soul and my necessity and urgency to release my truth. She pawned me off for a while but eventually she started to listen and put pen to paper. We headed to the Royal Irish Fusiliers Museum in Armagh to look for my army records and the research began.

**RESERCHING AT THE ROYAL FUSILIERS
MUSEUM IN ARMAGH**

Chapter Twenty

RETURN TO MALTA

It is true that you are never too old to change. By October 2010, during my ninety-first year and after sixty-eight years confined to barracks, I decided I wanted to return to the beautiful island of Malta. The prospect of looking at the four walls of home for another long winter did not appeal to me, so out of the blue, I decided a little excitement was what I needed. I just knew I was supposed to go to Malta and I was determined to find a way. I spent the best days of my youth there and I knew it so well. My wife did not like to travel, so I never thought of asking her to go, but now I was free so I asked Rosemary and Peter to take me. They applied to the Lottery for the, "Return for Heroes" funding and within a few weeks the flights were booked and we were off to the Mediterranean. I suggested a month tour of duty, but I got a week. My over-protective daughters were a little shocked by my impulsive behaviour and as I packed up my old kit bag and smiled, I told them not to worry. I let my granddaughters know that, unlike them, I was used to travelling light. Although the girls had never seen me travel before, it was a walk in the park for me, as I had been out and about long before they were even a twinkle in my eye.

A camera crew, including my nephew Owen and his son Eugene, along with my co-writer Mary organised to meet us for a few days of the trip to make a documentary of my return visit. I certainly was living the dream at last and the quiet wee Irish man was ready for action. Oh boy, my well-trodden path through life had taken many twists and turns in its time, but a film star was definitely a highly unexpected twist. Secretly I was very pleased with my new role and I said "Faugh Á Ballagh and Clear the Way." First I had to clear my way through the wind and rain at Belfast airport to get to the plane, but from there the flight was excellent, with comfortable seats and pretty hostesses, very different from the cargo hold of a Dakota or Lancaster bomber. But, as the pilot announced we had taken a route down Italy and over Sicily on our approach to Malta, I went numb for a moment as I pictured the enemy planes heading for the coast of Malta and me. Suddenly I thought I must be crazy to leave home again, but I quelled the irrational feelings and got back to the excitement of the present-day adventure. Never in my wildest dreams could I imagine that one day, in 2010, I myself would approach from Sicily in an aircraft. Thankfully I was not in one of those Stuka 88s, as I could never tolerate those pests.

We landed at night, so I had to wait for morning light to see my old island friend. At first light I pulled back the curtains to greet the morning sun over St. Julian's Bay at Sliema, only today I was in a beautiful hotel room instead of a dark miserable gun post. Even though the coast was lined was high-rise hotels and modern pathways, I recognised the ambiance and climate immediately. The sea and the smooth yellow rocks looked exactly the same and I imagined jumping into that warm comforting water. I had never swam since my time at the Suez Canal and I couldn't imagine Rosemary letting me go for a dip today. As I stepped outside I was thinking "oh boy, I have missed that heat on my back all these years." But as I stared out to sea, I could also envisage the horror of burning ships as air raid sirens roared in my ears, as the AA guns and Bofors pounded out their shells and as the JU87s and 88s flew past delivering their nasty gifts by the hundreds. The earth shook and I realised I was only lost in the mists of time.

Walking along the modern seafront, I was just a little unnerved by the flashbacks and, as if by magic, we came upon a newly built grotto to Our Lady of Lourdes. In an instant I relaxed, as my childhood feeling of being looked after washed over me and I knew this grotto outside my hotel was here to symbolise something good. Peter and Rosemary remained dumbfounded for a moment at the sight of the grotto. I was now ready to proceed with confidence as I was well accustomed to signs of hope. The following afternoon we met the camera crew in a sunny square in Valletta, just outside St. John's Co-Cathedral. Discreetly, Peter had bought a wheelchair and out here, away from home, I happily availed of its services for the first time in my life. As we travelled in from Sliema on the bus along Marsamxett Harbour, I caught my first view of Valletta and the little fishing boats still bobbing in the water. Of course yachts instead of warships now accompanied them, but the sight was familiar. As we drove through Ta' Xbiex, Msida and Pieta, the names just starting flowing off my tongue. Climbing the hill into Floriana we passed under the huge archways that had marked my journey to and from the city all those years ago. I felt like a lad again as the bus stopped at the enormous fortress walls guarding the entrance to Valletta.

The magnificent opera house that once greeted me, still lay in ruins just inside the gates and I noticed the walls still bore the scars of bullet holes. Otherwise my old friend was in good shape, compared to the day I left her in rubble. As I rolled down Kingsway, now renamed Republic Street, I soaked up the relaxed, happy atmosphere. At the café we had a delicious fish lunch as I talked intensely about my young life here to the camera and marveled that I was the one now sitting at this café, instead of standing down a side street eating sausage and mash. The cameras followed us down the steep hill to Fort Elmo to visit the War Museum at the point of the headland. As a young athlete I never realised the streets in Valletta were so steep and, to be honest, they were no bother to me at ninety-one either but the wheelchair pushers, at half my age, seemed to be quite unfit. Of course I had to stop at the Palace to watch the changing of the guard, and as we watched the soldiers, my daughter could not believe I too had moved as elegantly as these young lads. Many a day I had marched up and down Kingsway behind our Regimental band or stood at the palace gates and on St. Patrick's Day and Barrosa Day we had a special parade and the locals loved to come and listen to our excellent music. Our Regimental March was one hundred and twenty paces to the minute, therefore it is quite slow yet stylish.

Everything in the War Museum was familiar and I could explain the workings of most of the machinery. The remaining Gladiator plane 'Faith' had pride of place and my old 15-hundredweight truck brought back some memories. It was clear to see that my travelling companions seemed overwhelmed by the soldier who had invaded the body of Wee Packie, the quiet man from Omagh. I must admit I was altered for that afternoon as my expert knowledge of warfare seemed to burst out of some hidden cavern in my brain. Dates, names, places and long forgotten details simply presented themselves at the tip of my tongue, without a second thought. Rosemary was going around checking the details on the notice boards, but I was yet to be proven wrong. Once I had started on this process of speaking my truth I had great bother getting stopped, but I was in my element. The cameraman caught it all on film and I was so relieved he was there capturing my history. I was contemplating my quiet life back home and thinking I must have fallen into a sleep for sixty-eight years and now I had come to life again. That day was one of my best so far.

The next day we hired a car and I asked to go to the village of Mosta. The island has become so built-up and busy, but I recognised some landmarks and names. We passed through the little villages where the ordinary people had gathered precious money to buy gifts for the Royal Irish Fusilier Regiment in thanks after the war. Naxxar had presented us with a silver cannon. The kind people of Gargur had given us two silver cups as a sign of friendship between the Maltese and the regiment. And Mosta presented us with a silver model of a Gozo boat. All these gifts are proudly displayed in the regiment's museum in Armagh.

One of my main ambitions for the trip was to visit the magnificent church at Mosta. I was shocked, and I suppose disappointed at how the little village of my memories had mushroomed around the central dome of the landmark church. The last time I was so close to this impressive building was the night of the bombing. At long last I managed to get inside the Church of the Assumption in Mosta. They say there is a church for every day of the year in Malta and each one is more elaborate then the next, but this is the one I was drawn to, with its feast day on the 15th of August. On entering the building, I immediately felt a sense of calm and healing. The dome mesmerised me with its magnificent beauty of blue calm. A replica bomb is now displayed in the Church, as a testimony to the miraculous escape of so many people, including me. I remember watching those three hundred innocent people flood out through the doors that day towards a safer haven. I was not prepared for the emotions of this special visit and I lit a candle for Kate and also prayed for all of my many dead comrades buried on Malta and Leros. If only we had the protection of this dome in Omagh on the 15th August 1998. As Rosemary and I sat under that protective dome, a singer and a guitarist began to fill the church with music. The sound was haunting and then the words rose up into the dome and reverberated around us like a heavenly choir. The song was so familiar as I picked up the word, 'In the arms of the Angels, may you find, some comfort here."

Rosemary announced that it was the special song we had requested to be sung at her mother's funeral. I knew then that something extraordinary was happening around me and that Mary and Geraldine would most likely be involved. Those two were always organising and I am sure our souls don't change that much after death. That afternoon was the highlight of my trip. We drove through the area that was once Ta' Quli airfield and visited the Aviation Museum. On the way back to the hotel we drove up to my old home at Mtarfa Barracks on the hill. It had changed, but the view was still incredible and I could see how urbanised the island had become in my years of absence.

As the days rolled by, I was becoming more and more attached to my old home. I was rekindling an old love of the place and I remembered the island had stolen my heart once before. The people were just as friendly as ever, seemingly untouched by the rat race of the western world. They still had siesta in the afternoon and took the time to converse. I met so many people who wanted to shake my hand and thank me for being here during their dark days of war. They knew to call "Faugh A Ballagh" to me and I must say, I was enjoying my new role as a hero. Many other veterans had fallen in love with the island also and came back to live on Malta. I was now convinced I should have done the same, but Mary might not have wanted to leave her family. When I spotted all the red BT telephone boxes, I was sure they must have been easier to install here, than the ones I had worked on in the wind and rain of Tyrone and Fermanagh. I should have had that radiant sunshine on my back all year round, but then again hindsight is a wonderful thing.

For a man who never asked for anything in his life, it seemed strange to be the centre of attention. We met so many wonderful people keen to share their stories. I had my chest out and my head high, as I directed my little tour group around the narrow streets and along the country roads between the villages. When I drove these roads in 1943, they had contained a few more potholes. At the war memorial I fell in with a Canadian tourist who had come to see where his father had served during the war, and the locals told me about their childhood memories in the underground shelters. It is difficult to explain, but I felt alive and confident with the freedom to finally speak out in my true voice. We talked about my book and our wonderful holiday experiences and, as the final days drew in, I knew I was reluctant to leave my island home. I had so much more to do and the heat on my back was comforting. One place I had on my mind to visit was the graveyard at Ta'Qali, but we could not locate it. I also wanted to spend a day at St. Paul's Bay basking on the beach.

A week is not long enough for a holiday in Malta, I say, with my vast experience of holidays. I had high expectations as the last time I took a trip to the Mediterranean I stayed away eight years and came home via a grand European tour.

On the last day of filming we went to absorb the vistas of Grand Harbour from the Barracka Gardens in Valletta. 'That's a real graveyard down there' I told them all, as I had seen many vessels and fighter planes go down in that body of water, often with our food rations still on-board. Now, that is what you really call a sinking feeling. A loudspeaker in the park poignantly transmitted the voice of Vera Lynn singing "We'll meet again" and I was transported back through time. The rest of the day I was very reflective as I thought about my life and how different things might have been if I had stayed or returned here to Malta. My personality was enhanced and confident here. I loved the direct Maltese style of communication and the Mediterranean pace of life; yes, Malta suited my mindset perfectly. Thank God I had made this trip and found the healing I needed.

Overlooking Grand Harbour there now stands an impressive monument to the seven thousand lives lost on Malta from 1940 to 1943. It is a miracle the whole island did not sink with us all on-board. Malta truly deserved its title, as the unsinkable aircraft carrier. The lonely Siege Bell commemorates the awarding of the George Cross and rings at noon every day along with a cannon gun salute and the plaque states:

> *"This bell tolls in memory of those who*
> *gave their lives during the*
> *Siege of Malta 1940-1943.*

Situated beside the bell is a majestic statute of a Dead soldier, laid out respectfully on a slab above the harbour with a plaque stating:

> *"At the going of the sun and in the morning.*
> *We will remember them."*

I cannot explain how important it was for me to witness the respect the Maltese nation still bestowed on all these lost souls from so very long ago. They still remembered them every day. Maybe I had been cut off from my need to grieve the intensive loss of my youth, in a community who bore no sympathy, but here people understood and I felt their compassion. I had come to my Tír Na nÓg, drank of its healing waters and now it was time to return home.

PACKIE RETURNS TO MALTA 2010

Chapter Twenty-One

A MALTESE SEIGE

Well, now the story takes a very interesting twist. I am sure my Uncle Patrick would be very proud of my newly acquired story-telling abilities, but I really did have to endure the thrills and spills of my adventures before I could tell them. It suddenly dawned on me that maybe his so-called fiction tales could possibly have been real after all. I wished I could remember some of them now and I wondered if my uncle Patrick perhaps had been shipped to Malta for treatment during the First World War. I yearned for our long conversations and the stories he could have told about here, if his voice could be finally freed like mine was now.

On our last night, as we sat at our last supper in the restaurant, the heavens opened and Malta witnessed one of the worst thunder and lightening storms in a century. To be honest, we passed little remarks on the rain, being well hardened to the Atlantic downpours at home. But the locals seemed anxious about so much rain. We had a laugh as I had told everyone it never rains in Malta and we watched people take off their shoes, roll up their trousers and paddle out into the warm floodwaters. We toasted the success of our trip and retired for the night.

The next morning I woke early about 4am feeling hot and ill. Of course I went and took a shower, as I thought it was just a chill. Coming out of the shower I felt like I could neither sit, nor stand, nor lie, so I rang Rosemary in her room. When she came to me, I was on the balcony trying to get some fresh air. She immediately rang for an ambulance. The lightning flashed and the thunder rolled all around me and it seemed like old times.

But if I didn't panic in 1939, I will not panic now I decided.

The ambulance arrived, having battled through the extraordinary flooding outside, and off I went to hospital with a siren and flashing lights. With great speed and efficiency I was wheeled into the high-dependency unit and immediately I had about ten staff working on me. They were very reassuring, but the bed was in the middle of the floor and I don't like things going on behind my back. I also had no shirt on and for the first time in a lifetime my tattoos were on show and naturally attracted attention. I worked hard at staying alert in all the fuss, as machines bleeped and alarmed and needles went into my arms. This was a new situation for me as I had little experience of medicine since my stay in the German POW hospital in 1943 and that didn't exactly instill confidence. But I felt safe now as I listened to the Maltese chatter all around and the doctor and a kind nurse reassured me continuously in English. Within minutes, a priest gave me a blessing and the last rites and I relaxed a little more. My grandniece, Mary came in and joked with me by saying, "If you were so keen to try out a gas mask, you should have asked at the museum." I laughed under the huge mask on my face, as she knew I had carried a gas mask around with me throughout the war years but never actually got to use it. She also knew I wanted to stay longer in Malta and that I should have gone to hospital the last time I was here in 1943. At least someone knew my story now and it was saved for all time. I was content to see Rosemary and Peter nearby and I thought I would be okay. Meanwhile, the doctor kept constantly in touch with my family. He told them I was in heart failure and my lungs were full of fluid, maybe due to a heart attack even though I had felt no pain—he told them I was critically ill but that he would try his best. When someone remarked that maybe we should not have travelled, the doctor immediately asked if I had enjoyed my visit and, if so, that life is for living and, it is not about sitting around waiting to die. Well I agreed, because if that was the case, I'd have been waiting a long time.

I had been in tighter holes than this in my time so with prayers, modern technology and great medical staff, I started to recover. By lunchtime, the four of us had missed our plane and I was staying in Malta a little longer than expected. It was time to lift my head up and see how everyone else was coping. I told them that the last time I came to Malta I had to stay a bit longer than expected as well, so not to worry. By mid-afternoon, I was wheeled to a cardiac ward and settled in to stay. I was still wired up to machines, but feeling much brighter. The family stayed with me and we all began to calm down. One of the nurses attending me was called Claire Mulligan and her grandfather had been in my regiment and had married a Maltese girl. I also had a Nurse O'Neill who had a similar family background. The bed was comfortable and I settled in to sleep, knowing I was safe with the Maltese people. All the talk in the ward was about the severe floods of the night before and how an undertakers store had been swamped, washing the empty coffins out into the road to float alongside the morning commuter traffic. People were frantic as they thought the coffins had risen up from the cemetery and I had to laugh to myself and thank God I was not in one of those coffins today, floating out to my favourite swimming spot in St. Paul's Bay. If you don't believe me about the coffins look up the news for Malta 25th October 2010 and see for yourself. The Mater Dei Hospital is built between the towns of San Gwann and Birkirkara, not a stone's throw from the place where I took the bang on the head in 1943. It was as if I had a longstanding date with this spot and the weather had conspired to get me there. But it was not my day to die.

The hospital was ultra modern and very strictly managed and cleaned. They had a visitors' guard at the locked door to the ward and my ones called him the Rottweiler. I knew I was a safe as houses and the priest came every day with Communion to me, so all my needs were cared for. As the days rolled by I kept improving and Mary and I continued writing the book, to pass the time. We had a telephone and the Internet at the bedside, so research was simple enough and I enjoyed hearing my memories verified as facts in history. My two mother-hen daughters at home in Ireland could speak to me anytime with the phone at my bedside. I told them I was going to stay the winter in Malta and I would see them in March. I also told them I was considering going into Valletta, as soon as I got out of hospital, to get a new tattoo etched on my back saying: "I survived Malta 2010." They told me that once I was home I was never getting past the Dublin Road corner again. It was an anxious time for everyone, but we did have some great laughs. I had blood in my urine and when the nurse came I said to him "Imbid a□mar". Both of us had a great laugh and my ones thought I was confused. Rosemary looked for an explanation and I translated by telling her it meant "red wine." My daughter of fifty-nine years had no idea I spoke any Maltese. Well I spoke very little really and most of it was pub talk, but it was a good test for my memory. We rang home to Ireland for an ancient cure for bleeding and the urine turned clear. The next day I was able to say, "Birra" meaning "beer" to the nurse and we all laughed again.

Mary continued our research around the island in the mornings and reported to me in the afternoon. She finally found the graveyard at Ta'Qali and furnished me with photographs of the well-kept cemetery and the individual graves of my comrades Mooney, Donaghy, McCann, Burke and Gallagher. There was also Whelan, Byrne, Brown and McCauley; all aged less than twenty-five years of age. I was very pleased to see the headstone of Captain Connors, whom we buried in 1938. It turns out he was not aged at all, at only fifty-one years old when he died. He had a Celtic cross headstone with Faugh À Ballagh engraved upon it but bullet holes had damaged the marble in the subsequent war years after his death. My scout had gone to Ta' Quli Craft Village to buy gifts and on entering the Heritage Homes factory she met the owners who, in true Maltese style, sympathetically listened to her story of being stranded in Malta looking for a graveyard and kindly drove her to the gates of the military cemetery. I was not surprised at the Maltese kindness because I knew these men understood this mission was important. The Maltese have always appreciated the spiritual values in life. I think my family worried that my mission might have been about finding a burial spot in Malta, but I was only getting started with life and I was simply content with the sight of those young lad's names and knowing where they had found repose. Yes, the Maltese understood that having a respectful acceptance of death helps a person cope better with the job of living. They are a people of great faith and patience, having utilised suffering and persecution differently from the Irish by turning it to their advantage throughout history without loosing vital friendships.

Malta is smaller than most counties in Ireland, yet they can operate as an independent Republic within the greater European Union, but their geographical position will always be strategic and the Maltese know they will need friends. The facial features of the Maltese immediately reflect a diverse mix of Arabic, European and African races. The language sounds Arabic and the culture appears more European. The English and Italian cultures have strongly influenced the society, bringing a mixture of reserve and also excitability. Yet these beautiful people live in harmony despite strong personalities and differing opinions. In Malta, a spade is called a spade, but with a good sense of humour. As I lay in my hospital bed, I was happy as Larry, with an ideal lookout post on a busy ward to watch all these interactions and relationships at play. I am blessed with excellent hearing and eyesight, which is a wonder with all the noise and flashes my head has experienced in its time without goggles or ear protection. I love people and people came to speak with me so by the time my family arrived at noon every day, I could inform them of all the dramas and daily gossip. From my hospital bed, I was introduced to the Internet and at Hallowe'en my three granddaughters won a dress-up competition in Omagh as Barbie Dolls and I was able to see them online the next day. I realised I needed a laptop for home if I was to have any 'Street Cred (ibility)' with the grandchildren.

I must say, my stay in the Mater Dei Hospital was a very positive experience as staff, other patients and their visitors treated me with kindness and respect. I was finally released two weeks later, with a report of having made a very surprising recovery and I was back on holidays at a hotel for a week. On Remembrance Day, the 11th of November there was an additional cannon gun salute at 11 am and I secretly wished I might attend the Remembrance Sunday events at the weekend. This day is very significant in the Maltese calendar, with a parade along Republic Street to Mass in the Co-Cathedral, celebrated by the Archbishop and attended by government officials and veterans from around the world, followed by a solemn ceremony at 11 am at the War Memorial. It would have been a bonus to stay and attend, but Mary said she would go for me, as she had never experienced a Poppy Day event before. It was comforting for me to know that so many people in Europe and across the world still honoured the twenty million dead of World War One and fifty million, who sacrificed everything for our freedom in World War Two. In my homeland, hundreds of thousands of fallen Irish lads have been denied that respect by a national ignorance of what those wars were about. Whether they like it or not, most families from both communities will find an uncle, granduncle or long-forgotten relative who served as a British soldier. If they trace back their family tree, he will be there, but most likely he was never talked about. These souls need to be prayed for in their families and in their own communities, lest we forget they existed. Soon there will be no one left who actually remembers them. When I think of the lifetime of memories and emotions that Geraldine's life represented to us and of all the time and sympathy we received at the time of her death, my thoughts also go out to all those corpses I witnessed in Germany and how little comfort their relatives received. I also remember the young soldiers on all sides, buried where they fell. They got no burial ceremonies or words of comfort, many have no grave to bring flowers to and cry at. There was no public recognition at that time of a precious individual life lost.

In Malta, the people still understand the spiritual connection with their past generations and they appreciated the purpose of my journey there. I suppose many others had made the same pilgrimage, but fewer had returned in recent years. I talked about riding out the winter in Malta, until March, but the fish with me weren't biting and the two lassies at home demanded I come back immediately, even resorting to bribes of my favourite home cooked meals, which they knew I'd find difficult to refuse. As a last resort, they made offers to rub my head like they had in childhood when they wanted something. I knew I was far too soft and the women won again. The insurance company organised the flights home on Remembrance Sunday, so I missed out on the big day, but they sent a lovely German doctor named Stefan to accompany me all the way home to Omagh. The night before travelling, Stefan came to visit me at the hotel and I immediately knew I was in good hands. I tried out a little of my limited German vocabulary on him and he informed me that, wherever I had learned the language, my accent was quite polite. We then talked about my life in Germany and the fact that German doctors had saved my life the last time I was in hospital in 1943. The reading at Mass that night on the eve of Remembrance Sunday said:

"The Lord says: my plans for you are peace and not disaster; when you call to me, I will listen to you, and I will bring you back to the place from which I exiled you."

Jeremiah, 29:11

I resigned myself to go to that place I was exiled from, even though I was not sure I wanted to be exiled from Malta, but I knew I had to go home. Stefan took great care of both Rosemary and me on the journey home, giving me oxygen throughout the flight and I must say I felt very relaxed, even as we transferred in Heathrow. He had been a nurse before training to be a doctor, so he knew what he was doing. At Heathrow airport, a two-minute silence was observed in remembrance of all the dead of the World Wars and there, the three odd travelling companions sat, with an Irish passport, a British passport and a German passport, together in prayer. Stefan told me he would accompany me to Germany if I wanted to go back and I hoped I had not left it too late in my life.

A taxi was waiting to transport us from Belfast Airport to Omagh and bring Stefan back for his return flight home. I was so embarrassed and upset when we were diverted off the motorway in the fog because of a bomb scare on the road and Stefan subsequently missed his return flight home that night. I will never understand anyone thinking a bomb placed on a motorway aimed at joining the two sides of the border, could possibly achieve a military objective to unify the country. Maybe that is why I never was promoted to a colonel!!!

Once at home, I settled in to the family attention with ease, as my great grandchildren performed their Irish dancing jigs and reels around my feet and I told of my adventures so far. Well the kids were more interested in the dancing, so competition for the stage was stiff. I was back in the protective cocoon of my precious family and community, but my adventurous free spirit had now been released again. My heart had rid itself of the heavy burden of grief, fear and the conformity of keeping my head down. I had stepped out, put my head up and survived the wrecking ball of life, after sixty-eight years frozen in a defensive mode. With my heart no longer numb, I was finally free from taking the safe route through life and I was looking for adventure again. But my body was letting me down, just as I was ready to fly.

Chapter Twenty-Two

THE PRICE OF FREEDOM

I am now ninety-one years old and finally I have realised my purpose in life. Over the last four years since the loss of my wife I have been compelled to document my experiences, as testimony to the effect of war on one individual person, up close and personal.

As we watch the news today we hear a bomb went off in Iraq or somewhere foreign, killing any number of people and we may say, "Isn't that terrible", then forget about it, or maybe we think nothing at all. Looking at war from a distance, through the media, we experience no impact, hearing the news in a void of any real appreciation of the suffering as if we had just watched a movie or a soap opera. I have witnessed and experienced the suffering and the reality is more gruesome than imaginable.

I am not unique—war affects millions of human lives—but I realise I have seen conflict from many different angles. I have been a child of war, a soldier in battle, a prisoner of war and a bereaved civilian. I have survived war in its extreme intensity, witnessing human death by tens of thousands at a time, but I have also picked my steps through a conflict in my own homeland for most of my life and just when my guard was finally down my fellow countrymen stabbed me right in the heart. I seem to have many reasons for anger but I know avenging my loss by making someone else suffer will never change my history, but perhaps the way I respond will affect the future.

Anyway, from a distance who would be the rightful target of my vengeance? Who is my enemy? Is it only the guy who drove the car into Omagh that day in 1998 or is it the warlords on all sides, who incite our hatred against each other? Is it the occupying British nation or the Irish nation who abandoned us around the time of my birth? Is it the elders who taught our children with the passion of anger not suffering, about 1690 or 1916, the famine or rebellion? There is no easy answer, and the value of revenge itself is questionable. I can assume that many of those bodies I encountered in Dresden were entire families wiped out together by the Allied forces in an act of vengeance motivated by how the Nazis wiped out whole families in the concentration camps. All through history we keep revenging evil with more evil and an ever-increasing number of people get hurt, angry and revengeful. So who is my enemy, who should I attack? From a distance it is easy to blame the wrong person, especially if I judge people as a group, but up close, each individual is unique. They are not a group to hate at random. Once revenge is let out of the cage, everyone one is in danger and innocent people get hurt.

Throughout history, those who want war have organised and prepared young people for battle while the people who want peace have neglected to organise and educate the young for peace. Peace-loving people cannot be passive against a bully, peace can no longer be the quiet submission of one vanquished culture to the dominant bullying will of another just for sake of peace. Unfortunately, there will always be a need for armies to protect against aggressors, but managing an army requires great discipline with a very strict code of ethics to prevent the crossing of the line between protection and aggressive revenge. Revenge is an entirely out-of-control action that no army must be free to exercise. Revenge creates more and more aggressors and less and less understanding. But real change will only come when passive people stop hiding behind the curtains, turning the other way. Peacemakers must confidently promote an alternative route, which leads to equality and the right of every culture to celebrate, without abusing the other.

But how do we handle the past and heal the pain? Knowing the truth is an important first step, and through enquiries and tribunals, hopefully every family will get the answers they're entitled to, even though many of the answers will not be easy to accept. I believe truth will always find a way to the surface, if we have patience to wait. It is difficult to forgive and even harder to accept responsibility, but true peace will only come when all sides embrace change and admit and accept some of the blame for nourishing hate, either quietly within the home or overtly in public.

Looking back now, I can clearly see that Northern Ireland was facing the same difficult crossroads in 1998 as it faced in 1922, a crossroads between possible escalation into outright civil war, or compromise for peace's sake. Of course they do say history repeats itself and it always will if humans do not learn any lessons from the past. Well I guess by 1998 in Ireland we had learned but little, as history records show that although the majority voted for peace, the hard line bullies on both sides still wanted a pound of flesh. But the community of Omagh along with a growing groundswell of ordinary peace-loving people around the country and abroad, decided to stand up to these bullies and give them what they least expected and certainly didn't want. Yes, we gave them words of peace and hope for a better future. By our refusal to avenge or sink to their level, our community left the bullies outside in the cold on the fringes of society. The Nationalist and the Unionist people stood up together and refused to be drawn into a civil war this time. Celebrities, pop stars and world leaders gave us their support and ordinary people from all over the world poured messages, money and hope into our community. I personally thank everyone who sent us hope in those dark days and I admire anyone who dared to dream of peace and reject thoughts of revenge at that crucial point in our history.

In Omagh, we slowly recovered over the years, but the scars are visible everyday in many families around the area and in homes all over the country after years of hurt. In these subsequent years, the political issues have not yet been completely resolved and tensions do still simmer here and there. But my belief is one of hope; that we have learned to confuse the bullies with gentle resilience and refusal to take their bait. Omagh will always carry the scar of that bomb in its legacy, but that scar bears testimony to a people who understand that the soul is more powerful then the body and although we cannot prevent evil inflicting a wound on a body, we can chose to stop the venom entering the soul. Buddha tells us:

> ***When one person hates another,***
> ***it is the hater who falls ill—***
> ***physically, emotionally, and spiritually.***
> ***When he loves, it is he who becomes whole.***
> ***Hatred kills. Love heals.***

It was not until recent years and after Geraldine's death, that I remembered my own mother's words, warning me that I would lose a child. Life made me wait until I was eighty years old, to understand what my mother had suffered at the loss of four children and the fear of losing me. Somehow the gypsy lady's words had travelled through time to me, over sixty years later and those remembered words comforted me, as I realised her vision proved a greater power and wisdom exists outside of the painful reality of this life, therefore when in the days before my Mary died she told us she had seen Geraldine sitting on her bed waiting for her I believed it, even though I could not see her myself.

The words reminded me that, like my mother, I had to pick myself up off the ground and continue cherishing the living around me yet again. My mother had given us her love, even though she had lost her other precious children. She could have curled up and retreated from us in her sorrow, allowing the hurt to consume everything. But no, she gave us sunshine and song instead, protecting our young hearts from additional pain.

I had also met with this choice before in my youth. On the battlefield I had faced the dilemma of lying down with the dead or pushing on with the living. This choice must represent the greatest crossroads encountered in life, as after any trauma or loss, an individual, a community or a nation must decide to tread a path for the living or a path for the dead. I have stood on that threshold, feeling the strong magnetic pull towards anger, depression and revenge, but what of the consequences of that choice of direction? I had witnessed enough of that suffering.

Of course the other path is more difficult, as it forces us to stop our human instinct and turn down a path looking for greater understanding and to accept some responsibility for the underlying causes of hatred. I feel this is not a submissive or passive viewpoint, as I strongly appreciate the need for protection, but there is a thin line between protection and revenge. It occurred to me that, under Nazi rule, that gypsy lady, with so much vision, would have been wiped out along with all her unique race and I was glad I had suffered to save her. The bigger picture of the purpose of my life was finally revealed and I understood the value my small role.

THE MALTESE CROSS BY HERITAGE HOMES OF MALTA

If asked what is important or what I hope my life epitomised, I just think of the Maltese cross. The four arms spilt at the ends, like wings to form eight points on the cross. These points represent the eight diverse cultures and languages of the Knights Hospitalier, who lived as a multi-national group, working together for the good of the whole nation of Malta, yet respecting each other's unique individual cultures. There is a plaque in a garden in Malta that reads "United In Diversity" and I like to think that we in Ireland could all be respected as individuals, remaining true to our unique traditions, yet respecting all others. Then we could all look to the future with a clear vision of how to contribute to the good of the whole community and still nourish diversity. We also need to realise that, like Malta, we need the friendship and alliances of our neighbours for survival in times of global threat. No man is an island and this island is too small on its own. Malta learned this from its history, when in crisis they welcomed help, yet they embraced the new without sacrifice of their ancient unique culture.

The four arms of the cross remind me of our four daughters and their families, reaching out from us at the centre, towards their future, continually branching out, yet always remaining attached to Mary and myself throughout time. In 2011, all four branches will bear great grandchildren, as two of my grandsons are expecting babies and Rosemary and Geraldine will finally share grandmother status with Kate and Patricia. With this image of my family and my story recorded for their future, I am now confident that my life was significant and worth enduring all these years.

And most importantly, the Maltese cross symbolises my faith and my commitment to the eight heavenly virtues of truth and faith, repentance accompanied by humility, justice moderated with mercy, purity and my old friend endurance of persecution. These virtues are common to most religious faiths around the world and they challenge us to live by high moral ethics. I have attempted to live a pure and humble life and I do repent my sins and failures. I have shown mercy to others who have harmed me. In my effort to live a good life I have submitted to the will of God and endured my fair share of persecution by my fellow man. I have faith that truth and justice will prevail.

Looking back, I suppose the war years and the Omagh Bomb seem to dominate my story, but I did not let them destroy my life. Of course I must acknowledge and mourn those losses, talk and vent my feelings about them, but I won't let them suck up a lifetime of the precious happy times. I shared so many peaceful joyous years with my family. My career gave me great satisfaction and I was well respected in my community. I lived the good times to the full and I continue to enjoy and see the blessing of each new day. I have a responsibility to my children to show my pride and joy in them, as I share and celebrate their lives. Granted, I have lost loved ones and friends, but I was lucky to have them in my life at all. They certainly don't want me wasting precious time moaning. If God still wants me on this earth, fit as a fiddle and happy as Larry, I must have work to complete here. So I rise every morning, give as much cheer as I can to the people I meet and attempt to live every day to the best of my ability.

So maybe the old saying, "What doesn't kill you makes you stronger", is accurate enough and, in the long scheme of my life, there has been more good days than bad. I refused to allow the tough times to dominate and destroy the rest of my life with anger and self-pity, as I know that anyone I love, living or dead, wanted me to move on with the living. No amount of self-inflicted misery, regret, victimisation or revenge can change one moment of the past. Freedom can be bought at a huge cost, but remember that it is worthless if you sacrifice or enslave others in its pursuit and nothing can take the freedom inside your soul, unless you decide to sell it yourself.

After Words

Packie finished his book in November 2010 while recovering at home. He remained determined and positive, but over Christmas his health deteriorated and Patrick Mc Crystal departed this life at 4pm on Friday 7th January 2011. His family never left his side during his last months and he continued to keep his guard up and rally the troops until the very end. One hour before he died, Packie spoke his last words to his daughters saying, "Next year we will all go to Malta and stay the winter". The devilish twinkle of his teasing nature was in his eye until the moment he died. He had a well-deserved, peaceful passing surrounded by a loving family. During his last night, he told us he could see a lamp glowing in the distance and asked for us to ensure it had enough oil. It was the only irrational words he had ever spoken in his life. Or maybe not, because as we all stood around Packie's coffin during the wake the following day we were amazed when the priest read the following bible passage from Luke 8:16-17. It was like a message of comfort from him to us.

"No one, when he has lit a lamp,
covers it with a container
or puts it under a bed;
but puts it on a stand, that
who enter in may see the light.
For nothing is hidden,
that will not be revealed;

**nor anything secret, that will not
be known and come to light.**

On a cold, icy, winter morning, a large crowd gathered in a quiet country churchyard near Omagh for the burial of a much loved and special man. Walter Pancott's son and the British Legion ensured that Fusilier Patrick McCrystal had a proper military burial, with the regimental colours, his medals and beret resting upon his coffin. A solitary piper played a lament as Patrick's grandsons bore him to the grave and a bugler sounded the Last Post and Reveille, as he was lowered down beside his wife. In true McCrystal tradition the ceremony was not over until Danny Boy was played by the bugler and later sung by his grandniece Catherine McMenamin during the funeral meal.

> **Oh Danny boy, the pipes, the pipes are calling**
> **From glen to glen, and down the mountain side**
> **The summer's gone, and all the flowers are dying**
> **'Tis you, 'tis you must go and I must bide.**
> **But come ye back when summer's in the meadow**
> **Or when the valley's hushed and white with snow**
> **'Tis I'll be here in sunshine or in shadow**
> **Oh Danny boy, oh Danny boy, I love you so.**

Like his father and grandfather before him, Patrick was a modest man, but surely he would be proud of the wonderful ceremony that sent him on his adventurous way from this life. His family and friends had done him proud and in their hearts he leaves a legacy of honour and integrity. Patrick also ensured his legacy will endure the test of time by finally sharing his story
"Lest we forget" the lessons of our past.

Sources & Interesting Reading:

The lines from 'From Failure Up' by Patrick Kavanagh are reprinted by kind permission of the Trustees of the Estate of the late Katherine B. Kavanagh, through the Jonathan Williams Literary Agency.

A copy of Operation Green is located at the Military Archives, Cathal Brugha Barracks, Dublin.

Mark M. Hull, *Irish Secrets. German Espionage in Wartime Ireland 1939-1945*, Irish Academic Press Ltd. 2002.

David Irving "Hitler's War" London: (Hodder) 1977

Wehrmacht situation conference of 3 December 1940.

Dufferin and Clandeboye, Helen Selina Blackwood, Baroness, 1807-1867. *Songs, poems, & verses, by Helen, Lady Dufferin (countess of Gifford)*. London, J. Murray, 1895.

Danny Boy Written by Frederic Edward Weatherly
Fred E. Weatherly, K.C. Piano and Gown: London & New York, G. P. Putnam's Sons, 1926.

W.B. Yeats: "The Second Coming" *Michael Robartes and the Dancer*. New York: Macmillan, 1921.

Patrick Kavanagh, "From Failure Up". *The Complete Poems of Patrick Kavanagh*, Newbridge, Ireland, Goldsmith Press:1984

Lightning Source UK Ltd.
Milton Keynes UK
177087UK00002B/2/P